Who's Gonna Drive You Home?

Cyndi Liming

Copyright © 2022 Cyndi Liming

First Edition

All rights reserved. No part of this book may be reproduced or used in any manner without written permission of the copyright owner except for the use of quotations in a book review.

DISCLAIMER: This book is a work of fiction based loosely on the author's recollections of experiences over time. Some names and characteristics have been changed. Some events have been compressed and recreated, and some dialogue has been recreated. Any resemblance to actual persons, living or dead, or actual events is purely coincidental. Credit for chapter titles go The Cars.

Prologue

Go ahead, hit me, I thought while he had me pinned up against my locker with his forearm. *Then everyone will know our little secret. HIT ME,* I willed with my mind.

CONTENTS

Chapter 1: Let's Go 6
Chapter 2: Here She Comes Again 19
Chapter 3: Just What I Needed 30
Chapter 4: Bye Bye Love 36
Chapter 5: Magic 51
Chapter 6: It's All I Can Do 62
Chapter 7: You're All I've Got Tonight 71
Chapter 8: Moving In Stereo 82
Chapter 9: Hello Again 87
Chapter 10: Since You're Gone 99
Chapter 11: Drive 111
Chapter 12: Double Life 124
Chapter 13: You Are the Girl 138
Chapter 14: Shake It Up 142
Chapter 15: Let the Good Times Roll 152
Chapter 16: You Might Think 173
Chapter 17: Since I Held You 180
Chapter 18: Everything You Say 191
Afterword 193

Chapter 1: Let's Go

*"And I don't want to hold her down
Don't want to break her crown…"*

"So I'll see you after school," Viv said as we walked into school.

She was going to take me home at the end of the day like she always did. She drove her parents' Crown Vic. Beige. We thought it was the coolest thing ever. Looking back, it probably wasn't as cool as we thought, but the Crown Vic meant freedom. Her mom had a thing for glass spheres. She had one dangling from the rear view mirror. When the light struck it just right, it would cast tiny prisms all over the inside of the car. It looked like a daytime disco in there. Viv was only 3 months older than me, but already had her license. That's Viv for you. She's always on top of her game.

We were entering our little country high school building that, no joke, was surrounded by corn fields. We had an awful gravel parking lot which obviously had no parking lines, so everyone just kind of parked wherever. The building wasn't anything remarkable either. If you flew over it and looked down, it was basically a rectangle made out of tan bricks. There wasn't anything fancy about this place. There were rectangular windows, two rows in fact, in every classroom, which matched the lovely rectangleness of the building. The uniformity of it all kind of reminded me of a prison at times.

Viv is the one friend I have known literally all of my life. She called me "cinnie" when we were little. There were 4 houses between her house and mine. Our parents have photos of us together as toddlers. My favorite is the one of us sitting on each of her dad's knees. Me with my Asian eyes and pin straight, thin black hair, and her with her ocean blue eyes and brown hair. We both had bangs cut straight across our foreheads like all little girls in the 70's. We were probably 3 years old when it was taken. There's another funny one of her pushing me in a stroller. The photo still cracks us up. Little did we know that photo would foreshadow what our friendship would be like: Viv always being the one to take care of me.

The school day always seemed to drag on, especially when I'd go into Mrs. Frank's biology class. I never really knew what I was doing there. It seemed so above my level of intelligence. I could never keep up and nothing ever made any sense, probably because I was focused more on my social life than any of the nonsense she was teaching us.

Mrs. Frank was one of those older teachers. You know the type: old lady haircut with silver curls that didn't move, glasses, out of date dresses or polyester pants with a blouse, the whole bit. She was tall too, for an old lady. I wouldn't say she was kind, but definitely not mean. Intimidating? Yes. She was going to teach us and we were going to learn, except for me though. I did not learn. When was I going to use any of this anyway? It's not like I was going to become a science teacher or a doctor or anything. No way. Not me. I was going to become the next Oprah Winfrey and have my own talk show. That was *my* plan!

Mrs. Frank would do this dreadful thing when she would review for tests with us. She would go around the room and ask each of us a possible test question. I never knew any of the answers. Sometimes she would ask me the very same question when it got back to my turn with the hopes of redeeming myself, only I still didn't know the correct answer even though she had just told me a few minutes ago. I swear each time she got back to my turn, I'd sink a little deeper into my seat. None of this would have made me feel all that bad if it wasn't for Charlie. He sat next to me, so if I missed the question, he'd have to answer it. He'd always get it right too. That's not so bad either, but the way he would look at me and shake his head always got to me. Sometimes I'd get an eye roll or he would rub his forehead with frustration, but I definitely looked pretty stupid. Sometimes I could feel him trying desperately to will the correct answer into my brain. That never worked either. I simply could not learn in her class, even with the magic of Charlie's vibe being sent to me telepathically. I take that back, I learned two things: pseudo means fake, pod means foot. Don't ask me why I've always remembered that. It has never helped me ever in my life, but that is something I managed to remember.

Gym class was also a total drag for me. I was not athletic and was always the last to be chosen for team activities. I hated having to get dressed for gym in front of the other girls too. You would think by 10th grade, I'd be over that. We had to dress in front of each other since the 7th grade. I was very self conscious of everything. I was overly thin, barely had a hint of any breasts compared to my peers, and I was brown, unlike the rest of the caucasian kids at my school. I was just barely 100 pounds at age 15, and kind of tall at 5'4. I was often told that if I turned sideways, I'd disappear. Getting dressed for gym was just another thing that I would dread each day besides biology class. If it wasn't for Michaela, gym class would not be tolerable in the least.

Michaela was a newer friend. We hadn't hung out much, but the more I got to know her, the more I wanted to be around her. She acted as if we were the best of friends, even when we first met. She was always happy to be around me. She was cheerful all the time. Everything was fun when she was around.

On this day, she came playfully up behind me and threw her arms around my neck, just giggling away with her sandy blond curls brushing against my shoulder. Nothing was actually funny, but she thought it would be funny to come up behind me like that and startle me. I released myself from her playful hug and turned to face her.

"What the heck are you doing?" I said, noticing her eyes with surprise. She was pulling out her own mascara covered eyelashes.

"I don't know. My lashes are bugging me."

"Literally, you have like 2 lashes left on each eye!" I looked down and her fingers were covered in mascara. "You're weird," I said. She just laughed carelessly.

"Come to my house Saturday," she said, changing the subject. I'm having a party. You gotta come!"

Heck yeah I was going to be there! I was THE minority at my school, and awkward as hell. I was grossly thin, flat chested, had a bob haircut *with* a spiral perm mind you, and zero confidence. Here I stood, in front of Michaela Brown, who was asking me, of all people, to come to her party. You better believe I was going to figure this out!

"I'll be there for sure!"

"Awesome! Don't forget!"

Finally, the end of the day came and I met Viv back at the Crown Vic. Like clockwork, we would pop in the Cars tape and sing "My Best Friend's Girl" at the top of our lungs. In addition, we did the traditional long horn beep. All the student drivers in the school did this. You'd pull out of the parking lot into a line of cars, turn right and wail the horn all the way until you reached the end of the building. If you were fortunate enough to own a muscle car, you'd leave a nice tire strip on the road. The longer it was the better. The kid driving the car might have been small and puny, but this was a symbol of one's badassness. This strip laying, horn blowing tradition was especially fun if you were skipping school or legitimately got out of school early for an appointment. It was like you had been liberated from something awful. Of course you were going to celebrate. How do teens in farm country celebrate the end of another dreadful day at school? You beep your horn long and loud! If you were on the inside of the building, you'd cheer for the person that got out. The teachers hated this ritual because it was so disruptive, however it united anyone on that side of the building for a small moment in time.

  Viv and I drove past the corn fields and the old run down antique store that was never open. The storefront was all glass and you could see the shelves stocked full of useless junk that no one ever bought. After about 5 minutes we rounded the corner to our street. I saw Viv look in her rearview mirror, her eyes wide.

  "Crap. It's the cops."

  I felt the car lunge slightly forward as she pushed down on the brake using that instinctive move that we all do when we see the police behind us. She had to be speeding.

"I'm only going 5 over. What the heck?" she said nervously.

The police car kept getting closer and closer, siren blaring and everything. All I could think about was that if she gets a ticket, that meant no more freedom. I have this party to go to on Saturday and I'd need her to drop me off! I was pretty self centered. I didn't even think about the consequences Viv would have to face from her parents if she got a ticket. There was nothing in the world that meant more than Michaela's party. Well, at least in my 15 year old mind.

The police car was right behind us. Viv started to slow down and vere off to the right, in order to pull over and receive our fate. We were both sweating nervously and turned down the music.

Her car slowed to a complete stop. We pulled our seatbelts on quickly. In the late 80's, people didn't make much of a big deal about seat belts, but we thought maybe if we appeared to be rule followers, the police would go easy on us. Maybe they would even let us go with just a warning.

The strangest thing happened. When Viv pulled off to the side of the road, the police car sped right by us, fast, as if trying to get to an emergency situation as quickly as possible. Sirens were still blaring.

Hmmmph. That's odd. But our anxiety soon faded away when we realized that the police definitely were not after us. We looked at each other relieved and let out a deep sigh simultaneously. Viv grinned at me and cranked up the Cars. We picked up where we left off in the lyrics to "My Best Friend's Girl" as if nothing had happened.

Five minutes later, we pulled into my driveway, which was oddly full of police cars. My neighbor's house had police cars in their driveway as well. What was going on here? All sorts of things ran through my very imaginative mind.

Did something happen to my parents or my younger brother? Did someone die? Was there an intruder in my house? Was there a murder? The horrifying thoughts were running through my mind at full speed. Our homes looked just like the ones on the news when there was a murder or something. It took me only seconds to leave Viv's car in order to burst into my house. My mother was already on the kitchen phone with our neighbor, panicking.

"Beth, you need to come home. Something's happened. Come home. I'll keep the kids over here," she said in a serious tone.

In a matter of minutes, Beth got home from work to find out that her husband, who had been drinking, had run a man off the road with his truck. The man was riding his bike and her husband struck and killed him. He never stopped to find out if the man was okay. He just kept going and barricaded himself in his house.

This was all very strange. Nothing ever happens in our town. The last bad thing that had happened was when I was a little girl and the neighbor's cows across the street got loose. It was kind of funny to see my dad and all those other grown men run all over town to round up the cows, but never anything like this, and it was happening right next door.

Naturally, all the neighbors were out, standing around with arms folded, whispering to one another, trying desperately to see what was going on while also making up their own stories. Later, I saw Will, Beth's husband, in a dirty white t-shirt, wiry hair and long beard, get escorted in handcuffs into the police car. I saw the bike too, mangled and twisted in the back of one of the police cars. I winced when I saw it. Within a few hours, my mother discovered that it was one of her good friends that was riding the bike.

Later that afternoon I walked down to Viv's like I did most evenings. I was like family, so I would walk through the garage, always pausing to take notice as to how clean it always was. It always had the hint of fresh paint smell, yet I never recalled them painting it any time recently and I was there pretty much every day. Like, did her mom mop the garage daily or what? There was never any garage filth on the shiny gray floor. Her dad's tools were always so neatly organized as if he never used them, but he did. I mean, who keeps an immaculate garage? Viv's family did.

One hundred percent of the time I would be greeted by Viv's mom, who oddly, I'd always called her Mrs. Barnes, even though she was like my second mom. She'd say, in her very thick West Virginian accent, "Well, HI Sandy (accent on the "HI")!" My name is Cyndi, by the way, but the twang in her voice always made my name sound like "Sandy." I always felt welcome there. She had a smile, a REALLY big smile, and would talk to me in a sing songy tone. Mrs. Barnes would have the best sun tea ever made, fudge or homemade canned beets. I never liked beets, but hers were simply amazing. Her dad, as always, would be sitting in his rocking chair next to the sliding glass doors. The doors led to the patio that he built himself with a beautiful view of their backyard. The patio overlooked the woods and the yard would dip down creating the perfect sledding hill for Viv and me when we were younger. There were bird feeders all over the backyard, strategically placed. Mr. Barnes also had the same thick West Virignian accent even though they both had been living in Northeastern Ohio for years. He was a man of few words, but had an infectious laugh. He would say silly things all the time and crack himself up while Viv would roll her eyes. He could build anything. Most of the time I'd see him sitting in his rocking chair, looking outside with a smile. I think the two of them were pretty happy.

Their house was always quiet with the exception of the ticking from the grandfather clock. Her parent's must have had a thing for clocks. They also had a cuckoo clock, and both would go off at the quarter of each hour. The grandfather clock would go off at every quarter of the hour, but when on the hour, it would chime the amount of times as the hour that it was. So if it was 8pm, you'd hear its little medley and then the clock would chime 8 times. If you were having a conversation, you'd have to pause until it was finished, simply because the thing was pretty loud. I don't know how they slept at night. How did Viv sleep through the madness?

"Viv's on the phone again with Terrence. Have some fudge and sweet tea!" Mrs. Barnes said with her usual enthusiasm.

*Yaaaaaasssss....*I thought to myself. I sat down at the kitchen table and talked to Viv's parents about the day. I always found their kitchen table to be interesting. It was rectangular except the end that was away from the wall was rounded. The other end was attached to the wall. You could see out into their lovely backyard if you sat in the right spot. It wasn't that big of a table, really. There were only three chairs, which was enough for Viv's family since her brother and sister were much older and no longer lived there. Diagonally from that table was a much bigger table, next to Mr. Barnes's rocking chair, that nobody ever used.

"That's awful what happened to Beth, isn't it? Will will probably go to jail. I'll be collecting up some money from the rest of the neighbors and I'll be making some dinners for her and the kids. You think your mom will want to help out?" Mrs. Barnes asked.

This was the first time that I realized that people should help each other in times of trouble. You would think that I would just know something like this, but I didn't. My family never helped anyone. I mean, maybe my parents did, but I was never involved. I know it sounds awful to say that my "parents never helped anyone," but in this town, people didn't need help because nothing ever happened.

"Sure!" I said, not really knowing if my mom would want to help at all. I mean, at my house, my dad worked all the time. My mom would run my thirteen year old brother and I back and forth to practices. Dinner was always ready for us promptly at 5pm. My mom also had a day job as well. I just figured Mrs. Barnes would be in touch with my mom soon, so I moved on from that thought and mosied on over to Viv's room.

"I love you. Forever and always," I heard her say to her boyfriend Terrence of over a year. I swear I vomited in my mouth a little. The "forever and always" phrase at the end of every single conversation between the two of them made me a little ill.

Terrence was a pretty good guy though. He definitely earned the "Best Friend Seal of Approval." He was tall and thin which worked out great for him. He was our star basketball player. He had dark, curly, short hair and a mustache. He was no older than Viv and me and had a full grown mustache already. Terrence was not like most boys. He was romantic, charming and thoughtful at age 16. I imagine most girls probably had a crush on him, but he was loyal to Viv. He was smart, just like Viv. The two of them were in the National Honor Society.

"I'm really tired," I said, trying to get out of the football game that we were supposed to go to. "I don't feel like doing my hair."

"Oh come on. I'll do your dang hair. We're going."

"No really, I think I might be sick or something. I just want to lay down," I said.

"Well, lay down on the floor by the bathroom and I'll curl your hair," Viv demanded.

"Really? Are you serious? You're the best."

I did as I was told. I laid down, with my face on the hallway carpet. Viv heated up the curling iron and proceeded to hover over me as she put random curls in my hair. I don't know what I looked like, but I must have been somewhat presentable. I was just so tired from the week, and I didn't care what I looked like.

"You're beautiful. Now let's go!"

Chapter 2: Here She Comes Again

"When she's dancing 'neath the starry sky…"

It was your typical high school football evening, cool and crisp, but not uncomfortable. You could see the bugs flying around the stadium lights to stay warm. The smells of popcorn and hotdogs filled the air. There were lots of people there. The community revolved around high school sports. Not because we were good or anything, but simply because there was nothing else to do. Because I went to a little country school, mostly what you'd see at football games was a lot of Carharts, jeans, fingers shoved into pockets, work boots and a lot of standing around in a circle. Most of us didn't pay much attention to the football game.

When Viv and I showed up, we did the same. We found Terrence and his friends, and we too, stood around, in a circle in our jeans, but we wore, with pride, our dance team jackets. They were black mostly, and we felt like we were the coolest thing since sliced bread.

There is no way we were talking about anything of any importance in our little circle because I cannot remember one single detail about any of the conversations. All I heard was the marching band playing. "Gimme Some Lovin'" kicked in, and I remembered that my friend Michaela would be twirling her baton in front of the band. It must be half time!

"I gotta go," I said, excusing myself from whatever was going on in our little circle. "I gotta go see Michaela twirl. I promised I would."

I made my way through the crowd, found Michaela's mom and stood next to her to watch. She was dressed in her sparkling majorette outfit. She had a huge, confident smile. Every time she threw that baton way up in the air, my nerves would get the best of me. I thought for sure she would drop it, but she knew what she was doing, and she never dropped it. She'd catch a glimpse of me and flash that overly huge smile. She obviously couldn't wave to me, but I knew that she knew I was there.

Somehow, after several lies and alibis, I found myself at Michaela's house the next day, a Saturday. Her mom wasn't going to be home. I never knew a thing about her dad. I know that my Filipino mom would go crazy on so many levels if she knew that Michaela was going to have a party, with alcohol, by the way, without her mom being there.

As soon as I arrived, Michaela took me up to show me her room, like all kids do when a friend comes over for the first time. It wasn't anything fancy, but oh my gosh, the amount of clothes that girl had! She had so many clothes stuffed into her closet that the clothes that were hanging formed like this U shape which caused the clothes to literally bulge out of her closet. I started looking through it. It wasn't an easy task either. Since there were so many outfits stuffed into that closet, I couldn't really slide the clothes across the bar with ease to get a better look. Everything was brand name: Forenza, Outback Red, IOU and so much more. Literally, she had to have every cool outfit from the mall in that closet.

"Hey, can I borrow an outfit for the party?" I asked.

"Of course you can. Pick out whatever you want."

After leafing through practically the entire closet, I narrowed it down to this shorts outfit made by Esprit. The shirt was baggy and went past my waist. The left side was blue and the right side was black. It had shorts to match, but the opposite side was black and the other side was blue. I was overly matchy. The shorts were like biker shorts, only made of cotton. Not sure why I thought this was such a great outfit, but for whatever reason I felt pretty cool wearing it. I was big into brand names at this age, so it didn't matter if I looked strange. It was made by Esprit. You couldn't see the brand name anywhere on the outfit, but I knew it was brand named, and that's all that mattered.

I didn't really know anyone at the party. Kids were pouring in from other schools. I wasn't super outgoing, and Michaela couldn't possibly be by my side all night long, so I did my best to fit in. I found myself sitting on the couch next to some guy I didn't know. We chatted a little bit, and for some reason, I decided to playfully pull off his ball cap. To my surprise, condoms fell out onto his lap. I just kind of looked at him, stunned.

"I'm going to find Michaela. It was nice meeting you," I said nervously.

"No, don't go. Seriously. I don't know why I have these. It's stupid. Stay here."

"No, really, I should go," I said, feeling very uncomfortable."

"Look, I'm not going to like, use these on you. What are you, prude or something?"

I've heard that one before. My friend Charlie, from biology class, always told me how prude I was, like he would know. I guess I just looked like I probably was. I didn't know what to say, but I definitely felt like I was in an After School Special or something. Out of nowhere, some guy that I didn't know, came to my rescue.

"She's with me. Let's go."

And I did. He was tall and fairly good looking. He dressed nicer than most boys at my school. He had on a nice, button down, light blue shirt with a collar and baggy jeans. He had on his high school jacket, but I didn't recognize the school. I didn't know this guy either, but I definitely knew that I didn't want to be around Mr. "I keep condoms under my hat just in case" guy. I grabbed his hand, which was so weird since I didn't know him, and we walked outside. Also, not a good idea.

I was fifteen. What did I know? Here I was trying to get out of one uncomfortable situation, to find myself in a brand new uncomfortable situation.

"My name is Dean. What's yours?" he asked kindly as we took a seat at the picnic table. Michaela's house was set back away from the road and lots of trees surrounded it. It was kind of spooky out there. This "Dean" could do whatever he wanted to and no one would ever know.

"Cyndi," I said awkwardly.

"Geez, you're freezing. Take my jacket," he said, handing it to me. "I noticed that you didn't seem comfortable around that guy. I hope it was okay to come to your rescue."

"Oh yes, thanks. I just met him," I said, not really knowing what to say. I stunk at small talk!

"So how do you know Michaela?" he asked, sensing my awkwardness.

"I have gym class with her. You?"

"I met her at a football game when your school played mine."

How in the world did she make so many friends? I swear she knew everyone in the county. Dean and I talked all night long. He didn't do anything to hurt me or make me feel uncomfortable. It was weird how natural conversation came with him. In elementary school, I was painfully shy. By junior high and high school, I started coming out of my shell a bit, but not much. He was funny, charming and kind. Was he an angel, who came to rescue me from Mr. Condom Man? After hours of talking under the full moon, he had to go. We exchanged numbers in the strangest of ways. All we could find to write with was a thick permanent marker.

He said, "Here, write your number on my arm." So I did, in obnoxiously large letters. It would take days to wash off. But, there was no way he was going to forget me!

Once everyone left, it was time to hide all the evidence. Michaela grabbed a bed sheet and fanned it out in the middle of the floor. She told me to grab all the empty beer cans and throw them on the sheet so she could haul them off. I was shocked at how nonchalant she was about this. There was no way I could ever have a party like this at my house, let alone just toss all of the beer cans onto this sheet. I mean, my mom would kill me once for using the sheet and then twice for putting the cans on it. She'd kill me a third time for having a party. There were cans everywhere, and not all of the cans were completely empty either. Beer definitely dripped out onto the sheet and onto the carpet. How could Michaela be so calm about all of this? Clearly, it was not her first party. But wouldn't her mother be able to tell? Her calmness was so intriguing to me. Michaela was all about fun with no thought of ever being caught. It was baffling, but I knew that everything about her was fun, and I wanted to be part of it too! When I went back to school on Monday, a boy I barely knew came up to me during study hall.

"I heard you are friends with Michaela Brown. You should stay away from her. She's a liar and a bitch."

First of all, you have to understand, everyone knew everything about everyone. This guy, that I had seen around school from time to time, but never spoke to, knew I was at that party. He wasn't there. How did he know? Why did he hate her so much? He didn't give me much detail other than that. I think he might have liked her and she didn't like him back, so he was going to drag her name through the mud.

"Just leave me alone. You don't know what you're talking about," I said.

I couldn't imagine how anyone could hate Michaela. She was super nice to everyone. She could talk to anyone, a skill I never had. She had friends from all over, so she couldn't possibly be that bad of a person. She was beautiful too. She could have dated any guy she wanted.

"You'll see. Don't trust her," he said, and walked away.

Over the next few months, Michaela and I spent tons of time together, which was good for me since Viv was always with Terrence these days. Michaela was at my house so much that eventually she called my mom, "Mom." She'd even go into the refrigerator without asking and help herself. Again, why was she always so comfortable? Viv had been my friend my whole life and I still called her mom "Mrs. Barnes."

We would talk about everything and anything. We were going to be photographers in California when we grew up. I was going to marry Luke Perry who played Dylan from the TV show Beverly Hills 90210. She was going to marry Jason Priestly. We were going to live in the city and go to college together. I loved talking about what our apartment would look like and dreaming about the fun we were going to have together!

One afternoon we went to Rax. Rax was our favorite fast food restaurant. Michaela was a year older than me, so she could drive the two of us around, which made her even cooler in my eyes. Her boyfriend from another nearby school, Scott, and his friend Toby, met us there. I barely knew either one of them. I saw Scott at the party and she introduced me to Toby when he got there. We were at the counter waiting to order.

Remember how Michaela thought everything was funny? Well, she did something to me that I will never forget. She depantsed me. This means that she pulled my pants down in front of the two guys we were with and all of Rax. Naturally, her infectious laugh echoed through the restaurant. I, on the other hand, was mortified! As quickly as I could, I pulled up my pants and gave her a glare. She was cracking up so hard and giving me the blue puppy dog eyes that I couldn't stay mad for long. Embarrassed, I took off to the restroom. I immediately went into the single stall.

"You're not mad are you, Cyndi? I was just messing around."

"I guess not. I just didn't think it was as funny as you did," I said embarrassed, definitely not wanting to stay mad.

"Well come on out, I gotta go pee!" she squealed.

"Just give me a second, geesh!"

"But I really gotta gooooo!" she wailed.

After a minute or so, I walked out of the stall to see Michaela, pants around her ankles, peeing in the sink. She looked at me and we both just started cracking up.

"You are crazy! Get down from there!"

"I told you I had to go!" she laughed, barely containing herself and clearly not caring if someone walked in.

After the Rax incident, we went to my house. Often Michaela would call her friends from other schools on my phone, and I would get to know them too. I had the coolest phone. It was a Swatch brand phone and see through. All of the inside parts were brightly colored. In addition, the base of the phone could become a receiver as well, so we could both be on the phone at the same time in the same room. I loved my new friend. She thought I was pretty cool too, and no one, other than Viv, really saw me that way. It felt good to be her friend.

One day, my mom came into my room and showed me the phone bill. It was oddly very high. Back then, we only had landlines, no cell phones like today. If you called beyond the city limits, the phone company would charge you by the minute. We were always on the phone for hours.

"Look at these phone numbers. Do you recognize any of them? Do you know anything about this? I think Michaela is calling people long distance from our phone." I looked. The bill was well over $300.

"What?" I had no idea. I knew we would talk to her friends from other schools, but I had no idea it was costing us extra money. In fact, I just assumed that the numbers were local and not long distance.

"Well, you are grounded for 2 weeks. No phone. No going out. No Michaela."

Grounded? What did I do? This was going to be misery. The thing is, part of me had this feeling that maybe that boy that I saw on Monday who said she was a bitch was onto something. Maybe she was a liar? Was she using my phone because her mom didn't want her to use her phone to make all of these long distance calls? Was she using me?

Hurt came over my body and I was starting to feel hot and dizzy. I was getting a sick stomach. I swear a knot was forming. I felt as if I was being punched in the stomach. How in the world could things be going so right for me and now it was all being taken away? I had done nothing wrong! I had this great new friend who made me feel like I was cool! I liked making all of these new friends from other schools and hanging out with Michaela. What was I going to do? I was so angry. How could she betray me like this?

I was still friends with Dean and we would talk until about 2am on the weekends. See, I was still grounded from the phone, but we had this system where I would call the time and temperature. Yes, that was a thing in the late 80's. The number was 246-1234. I would call it repeatedly around midnight and Dean would know to call my number. This way, the call waiting would pick up his call and the phone wouldn't ring and wake my parents. It was genius, really. I mentioned my new situation to him.

"You've known Michaela longer than I have. Would she do this to me?" I asked with concern.

"Maybe. The girl loves to talk, you know," he replied.

"Well what should I do? I am so angry that I got into trouble because of something she did. You know what? I think I'm just going to stop talking to her," I resolved.

And that was that.

Chapter 3: Just What I Needed

"I don't mind you coming here and wasting all my time…"

    I told Viv what was going on with Michaela. She started including me on her dates with Terrence once I was ungrounded. Since Terrence was friends with Charlie from Biology class, he tagged along too to "entertain" me.

    One night, we all decided to hang out at Charlie's house. He didn't live with his mom or a dad. He lived with his grandmother and brothers in a small white house. Nothing in the house was fancy, and many things were out of place--dirty dishes here and there, cups half full from the day before, cereal with a few flakes and milk sitting on the kitchen table leftover from breakfast. I knew his dad existed somewhere in the country, but I never heard any talk of his mother. He had a buzz cut, so he always had this sandy brown tuft of hair on the top of his head. If he grew it out, it would probably be horribly frizzy. He was a little taller than me and usually wore a faded concert t-shirt and jeans that were a little too tight. He had blue eyes, not like dreamy blue eyes, but kind of a faded pale blue that probably saw a lot of things a 15 year old boy should not see. For his age, he had a solid build. I don't know if it was natural or if he lifted weights. He looked like a total badass with a constant smirk on his face, like he might say something either smart assy or perverted. I knew I annoyed him a ton in Biology class. Here I was stuck with him in his basement while Terrence and Viv had some alone time. This could be interesting.

His basement was dark and full of your typical basement things. It was dark and a little musty with the scent of fabric softener lingering in the air. There were boxes stacked all over the place, and an old dirty rug on the floor. The washer and dryer were down there too. Tucked away in a dark corner was Charlie's twin sized bed with old blankets in a bundle strewn across it. There was a TV down there. Thank God for that. The background noise definitely made this experience a smidge less awkward.

I sat on his bed, since there was nowhere else to sit. He sat across from me on a stack of boxes. He lit a cigarette. Oh Lord, where is this going? Looking as cool as James Dean, he asked me if I wanted one, probably just trying to not be rude.

"No thanks," I said.

We sat there while he puffed away, not really saying anything. I just kind of played around with my fingers in the somewhat silence. At least the TV was making some background noise.

"You want a drink?"

"Sure," I said.

"Here." He handed me some kind of purple stuff in a bottle, definitely an alcoholic beverage. I thought maybe he would hand me a Pepsi or something. The half full, glass bottle said "MD" on the front. I took it in my hand and gave it a sniff.

"Ew!" I said. "How can you drink that? It smells like vomit!"

"Don't knock it til you try it, prude," he said.

Why was he always calling me that? We didn't know each other well, but we had the same circle of friends. It was a pretty bold adjective to use for a girl he only knew from biology class.

See, with Michaela barely my friend anymore, I needed to fill that gap. I wasn't going to her cool parties any more. We weren't hanging out. Her friends that she knew before me were starting to become a pain in my ass. Somehow I needed to fit in. I took a drink.

It tasted like I had eaten a bunch of grape Jolly Ranchers and threw them all up, and then drank it again. My face immediately started to feel warm and I felt this odd sensation move through my eyes and to my head. I must have made a sickening expression. Charlie, still casually puffing on his cigarette, found the whole thing to be very entertaining. He sat there, watching ,smirking and shaking his head.

"You're such a goody-goody. I'm going to start calling you Reverend," he laughed. "No, better yet, I'm going to call you Reverend Mother Sister Cyndi." He thought this was the most hilarious thing ever. "No, I got a better one. I'll call you Reverend Mother Sister Cynthia the Prude Nun. How's that for a nickname?" he said, laughing at himself hysterically.

He thought he was so clever. Well, I was going to prove him wrong. I kept drinking the grape vomit, each time wincing at the taste while also trying to keep my dinner from coming back up my throat.

We continued to watch TV while occasionally making small talk. He kept lighting his cigarettes and took turns drinking the grape Mad Dog with me. *Where was Vivian, dammit?* The room was starting to spin, my stomach was feeling lurchy, and I was feeling hot all over.

Charlie continued to say something, but everything was kind of blurry and moving in slow motion. In my mind I kept hearing "Reeeeevvverend Mooother Sissssster Cyndi the Pruuuuude Nun" and seeing Charlie laugh and laugh. I couldn't hold it down anymore and yes, you know it, dinner came up all over my shirt. I was too out of it to even bend over and vomit on the floor. Who was laughing now?

When Charlie saw how this was going down, he held back my hair while my body finished ridding itself of this poison. I could still hear him snickering and I could feel him rolling his eyes, just like he did when I'd miss a question in class. This definitely was not funny to me. When it was all over, I spit out one last chunk, and gave him this apologetic look. I shrugged my shoulders.

"Sorry," I said.

He just rubbed his face in mild frustration, a gesture that was all too familiar to me.

"Come pick out one of my shirts. You can wear this one or this one."

He held them up for me. The one shirt was a black Ozzy shirt with the image faded. I'm pretty sure it was one of his favorites because I recalled seeing him wear it frequently. The other, also faded, but tie dyed, had the Led Zeppelin logo on the front.

"That one," I said, pointing at the Led Zeppelin shirt. I wasn't a huge fan of Ozzy, but I loved Led Zeppelin. Plus, I didn't want to borrow his favorite one. I went around the corner and put it on. It was too big, but it was much cleaner than the shirt I had on. I made a mental note to throw it in the laundry at Viv's house.

I felt a little better after purging the grape poison from my body. Charlie never once seemed all that concerned, but kind of more expecting like this would probably happen. He let me lay down on his old lumpy twin bed while he cleaned up my mess and then continued to drink and smoke by my side. I must have fallen asleep. All I remember was Viv waking me up and telling me she was taking me home by my curfew, midnight, so that I wouldn't get grounded again. When we got in the car, she realized I still had on Charlie's T-shirt.

"What's up with that?" she said, pointing at my shirt.

I explained to her what happened and she rolled her eyes. Like Charlie, she thought it was kind of funny. I felt better after my little nap. She tossed me a cassette tape.

"Here," she said. "Put this in."

It was Led Zeppelin tape #4, song #1. As soon as I heard the all too familiar lyrics, I turned it up!

"Hey hey mama said the way you move, gonna make you sweat gonna make you groove," we sang at the top of our lungs while I played air guitar.

Chapter 4: Bye Bye Love

"Substitution, mass confusion, clouds inside your head…"

Monday rolled around like an old familiar friend. Speaking of old friends, when I was walking to my locker through the very crowded hallway, Michaela walked by.

"Cyndi, please tell me what I did. Why are you doing this?"

I should have just faced the uncomfortable question head on, but I was a coward. No one teaches you how to deal with girl drama. There should probably be a class on that. Thankfully the hall was crowded so I was able to keep moving.

I made it to my locker unscathed, or so I thought. My locker was off the beaten path. I went about my business, and out of nowhere, this guy, Tim, shoved me against my locker. He put his forearm across my chest as if that was necessary. I wouldn't be able to go anywhere with his big body making a wall in front of me.

Tim tormented me since I was in first grade. He was a football player and had some kind of vendetta against me. He always had something to say about how I looked. I bothered him for some reason, even though I had never in my entire life initiated a conversation with him. He was way bigger than me. He was tall with a football player build and broad shoulders. He towered over me. I never understood why a guy who hated me this much would spend this amount of time tormenting me. Isn't it really bad for a guy to pick on a girl who is probably half his weight? His tan colored hair was the same color of his skin and so it all kind of blended together. I remember thinking that his skin looked a shade of olive green. He had squinty eyes, a pointy nose like an owl and thin lips. When we were younger he would make these weird sounds when I walked by.

"Ching chong, ching chong." he'd say obnoxiously. This would mostly happen on the school bus to and from school when we were younger. The bus driver was aware and seated the two of us in the first and second seat, you know, to keep an eye on us. Tim knew there wasn't much she could do since she was driving, so he constantly said awful things about the way I looked. He'd speak to me in mock Chinese like I would understand the hideous meaningless noises he would make.

Everyday he'd say, impatiently, "When are you going back to your own country?"

Do you know how confusing that question is when you are 6 years old? I was born and raised in Ohio for crying out loud. It wouldn't be until later that I figured out how different I was from all the other kids. I never knew I was different until I started going to school. My mom would braid my hair in two tight braids. My bangs were cut straight across my forehead and I had really thick glasses and slanted, Asian eyes. I was a target for sure, but we were in high school by this point. How long was this going to go on? Thankfully Viv took me to and from school, so I was able to avoid Tim's daily tormenting on the bus.

So there I was pinned up against my locker. No one was around.

"Name 3 songs by Led Zeppelin," he said angrily, eyes full of rage.

I looked down at my shirt. I had forgotten that I was wearing Charlie's shirt over another shirt so that I could give it back.

"Uhm, okay. Stairway to Heaven…"

"Doesn't count!" he commanded.

"Uhhhh okay, uhm, Black Dog? Dyer Maker? Tangerine? Will that work?" I said nervously. His eyes were wild with rage.

Go ahead, hit me, I thought while he pondered his next move. *Then everyone will know our little secret. HIT ME,* I willed with my mind.

"You're lucky," he said disgustedly, and released me. "You don't belong here, Ching Chong."

What was he going to do if I couldn't name 3 songs by Led Zeppelin? I had to shake it off because I had bigger fish to fry. I took a few deep breaths to calm myself. Dance team practice was after school and Michaela would be there.

There was so much tension between us. I had managed to avoid her all day everyday. I don't know what she was telling her friends. They were bigger and meaner than me. They started glaring at me in the halls when we'd switch classes, and started yelling random obscenities at me throughout the day. Often, in the mornings while I walked to my locker, I would encounter a few of them standing in a circle, chatting before the bell rang. Sometimes they would call me names as I walked by, other times they would shove the person in their circle that was closest to me into me and knock me over. Sometimes I'd fall to the ground, other times I'd bump into someone else. Everyday my anxiety was going through the roof. I went from the weird looking skinny Asian girl to Michaela's new best friend to now an enemy to all of her friends in the junior class.

Dance team was always tense for the entire squad. Everyone knew Michaela and I hated each other. For the record, I never had the courage to tell Michaela why I was angry in the first place. Things had spun so far out of control that even I had forgotten why I was so upset in the first place. She was making sure that every day was torture for me. I never got my friends involved. Her friends were all big too, so every moment, from the hallway to gym class to lunch was somewhat terrifying. I had managed to avoid Michaela at all costs, but avoiding her friends was impossible. They seemed to be strategically placed wherever I was going to be, ready to pounce with their words and shove me around. The only thing I had done was not talk to her. And avoid her. And not tell her why I was doing any of it. Looking back, that is pretty bad.

I had never had to deal with girl drama quite this severe, so I had no idea how to go about it. Viv and I never fought. I take that back. When we were 6, we would play Dukes of Hazzard and she always got to be Daisy Duke, which enraged me. She had long brown hair, blue eyes AND was Caucasian. There was no role for an Asian girl with thick glasses in the Dukes of Hazzard, but I digress.

What I did to Michaela was wrong. If I could take it back today, I would. But because of my immaturity and lack of coping skills, I caused all of this. At the very least, I owed her an explanation, but so much time had passed.

Then one day, it happened. Michaela found me. She totally caught me off guard. I knew if I made the first right down the hallway, I would never see her, but on this day, she was onto me.

"Here, bitch," she said and threw a double sided, single spaced, handwritten note at me. Written in blue ink, I immediately recognized her handwriting. My friends and I opened it up. At one glance, all I saw was "bitch" this and "bitch" that. My face was getting hot and everything around me was becoming a blur. Even though there were lots of words all over the folded piece of notebook paper, I saw no other words on the page other than "bitch."

A passerby wanted to see what we were all looking at. She peered over our shoulders to get a better look. She said, "If I was you, I'd go in there and kick her ass."

That was just the permission that I needed. I think Satan himself entered my body. All of the hurt and the bullying and the name calling was coming to a head, ready to explode. I took the note and frantically tore it into pieces. I kept the pieces in my hand as I followed her into the lunch room.

I glanced around the room and my eyes fixated on her. There she was, by the milk cooler, with the leader of the Cyndi Hater group. Her name was Tracy. She was about a foot taller than me. Although she was a girl, she was built like a football player. She had long, brown hair and a spiral perm. The sides of her hair were pulled up high into a half pony-tail, complete with a scrunchy. She had mastered the mall hair bangs. To get successful mall hair, one must take a round brush to their bangs, pull it straight up towards the ceiling, spray it with a ton of Aquanet and then blow it dry. It's like a claw of hair right above the middle of the forehead. The mall bangs made her appear even taller and more ferocious, and she always seemed to have this disgruntled look on her face. Tracy didn't see me coming until I was right in front of her. She had no time to say anything to me because somehow my 100 pound body had managed to shove all of her probably 200 pounds out of my way. My adrenaline was working at full force. She gave me a dirty look but didn't dare get involved. I think she understood that this was going to be bad.

Everything started happening so quickly. I took the note that I tore up and threw it in Michaela's face, followed immediately by a right hook to her left eye. I was moving with unexpected lightning speed. The punch to her face even drew blood. I could see it trickle down her left cheek bone. She was stunned to say the least. She tried to push me away, but I caught a good chunk of her hair and started slamming her head into the milk cooler. My strength was a surprise, even to myself. I never knew what I was capable of. I slammed her head into the cooler once with a good blow, pulled her head back and went for another when suddenly I felt my own body being pulled away. It took me a few seconds to realize what was going on. It was my history teacher. He was breaking up the fight. I could tell that my body's strength made it difficult for him to tear me off of her.

He was dragging me out of the cafeteria by the back of my sweatshirt. He had a tight grip on the collar so much that it was twisted, tight around my neck. I kept trying to walk with my hands clenching my collar so I could breathe, but instead, all I could do was clumsily trip over my own feet as he was pulling me out of the cafeteria while everyone stood staring at me. I looked around and students crowded around us to watch. Kids were standing on the tables and chairs just to see. I had been humiliated all of my school life, but it was because I looked different from everyone else. Now, I was humiliating myself by my own actions.

Mr. Alden led me to the principal's office and sat me in the chair across from Mr. Lindon, the principal's desk.

"Stay here. Mr. Lindon will be with you in a moment," he said sternly.

Finally I was alone. As soon as he slammed the door, I started to cry. Not really a cry, but more like a wail. Tears were running uncontrollably down my face, covering my hands and shirt. It was one of those awful cries that one makes where they can't breathe. Oddly, it felt good to release the tears.

I was humiliated and sad and angry. so many awful emotions were going on at once. Mr. Lindon took a seat behind his desk across from me and asked me what happened. All I could do was gasp for air. My body was making that painful, quick inhaling sound. It was kind of like hiccuping, only I was just trying to breathe. After a few moments, I was able to calm down enough to speak a few understandable phrases, in between gasps.

Again, he asked, "What happened?"

"I don't know," I said, still trying to breathe normally. "We were best friends and then we weren't and her friends kept picking on me. I just had enough. I'm sorry."

I don't know why I felt like I needed to apologize to him, but I kept saying it. I was sorry. I was sorry for everything. I was sorry that I was such a coward and just couldn't simply explain to Michaela why I was mad at her in the first place, so many months ago.

"I know you have never been in trouble before, but I have to suspend you from school for three days. Your mom is on her way to pick you up."

Great. When was this going to end? I was living the Terrible No Good Very Bad Day story. I never told my mother about being picked on. My mom is super overprotective. I knew that if I ever told her, she would take matters into her own hands and that would have made my life even worse at school. My mom couldn't be around to protect me all the time, so I never told her.

I got into the car and stared out the window. We drove in silence. I had never longed for silence more in my entire life. I absolutely did not want to talk about this. Thank God my mother had decided to stay quiet. It literally was the best thing that had happened to me all day. It was kind of like a break!

Once I got into the house I went straight to my room, laid down and pulled the covers over my head. I think I seriously thought that if I stayed this way, I could just disappear from all of this madness. I didn't eat that night or shower or even change my clothes. I stayed like this until I eventually fell asleep. I was safe like this. The next morning, my mother came into my room.

"Maybe you need to take karate lessons," she said, with a hint of sarcasm. Anyone who has a Filipino mom knows that they have a way with words. They often say things without realizing how it may sound to the other person. Yes, let's do that. Then I will appear to be even *more* Asian. I was trying my best to blend in! I don't know why, but I leapt out of my bed in a rage, my fists clenched.

"JUST LEAVE ME ALONE!" I said.

"What, are you going to hit me next?" she said calmly, but accusingly. See what I mean?

I had no intention of hitting my mother. I was just still so angry and confused and PISSED because I had to come out of my safe little cave I had made for myself in my bed just to answer her question. I stormed off into the bathroom. Maybe I could wash the world away down the drain into my shower.

Coming back to school wasn't as nearly as bad as I thought it would be. I would see Michaela and her friends out of the corner of my eye in their usual spot by the lockers right by the front door of the school. This time, no one said a word. No one shoved me. I made it past them without a problem. I even passed Tim in the hall as well. He smirked at me, but actually said nothing.

Did that horrible fight scene in the cafeteria 3 days ago make people afraid of me? Doubt it. I don't think people were afraid. I mean, I was under 100 pounds. I think my message was conveyed: I had enough and I wasn't about to put up with it anymore. Was it possible that I could just blend in like everyone else for once in my life? As embarrassed and as sorry as I was for it even to happen in the first place, if it got people off my back, then it was worth it. Could I manage to make it all the way through the rest of my high school career unscathed?

Everything was pretty normal. I went to gym class. I stayed by my friends and Michaela stayed by hers. No one even gave me their daily dirty looks. Biology went just fine. Since I had been out for 3 days, I really didn't know what was going on. I couldn't answer any of the review questions, but this time, Charlie cut me some slack. Mrs. Frank even offered to tutor me after school to help me get caught up. As dreadful as that would be, I took the help.

Lunch was pretty normal. Well, I guess I should say abnormal since "normal" meant having to eat my lunch while also worrying about who was going to bump into me today and cause me to drop my food. One of my friends, Samson, got suspended again while I was out. For whatever reason, he still insisted on coming to school, well, at least for lunch.

He thought he was so clever. No one noticed he was there, not even me at first, until an orange drink flew through the air and hit my friend, Felicia, who was sitting next to me. Not sure if he was aiming for me. If he was, it was to be funny, which, he had a really strange sense of humor. Samson would never bully me. Felicia, on the other hand, didn't think any of this was funny. She had on a white shirt that day, and now it was covered in generic, cafeteria brand orange drink. She stood up, livid.

One of the lunch duty teachers happened to see what was going on. Samson, who couldn't help himself, continued to laugh and laugh. He was leaning back and forth and even put his head down on the table to try to contain himself. He was trying to hide, but failed miserably. The teacher escorted him out of the cafeteria, and he got yet another 3 days of out of school suspension.

I managed to make it through all of my classes with no one bumping into me purposely, and no one called me awful names. Tim and his gang of friends did not pull the corner of their eyelids towards their ears to make fun of my almond shaped eyes when they walked by. Oh my goodness, was this what it was like to be (gasp) white? This was heavenly.

Over the next few weeks, dance team became a little more normal, even pleasant. Michaela and I would almost talk to each other, but then remembered that we were supposed to hate each other, so we would carry on.

Our last dance team performance was coming up that Friday night at the varsity basketball game. We had been working hard for weeks on the last routine. It was going to be a real hum dinger too, let me tell ya. Since we went to a country school, it was our tradition to choose a classic country music song. It was such a big deal that if the townspeople saw us out and about they would ask us, "What's it going to be this year? El Vira? George Strait? The Judds?" I loved keeping them guessing and often would say, "Make sure you come to the game this Friday night and find out!" It was top secret until game night.

The night of the last basketball game of my sophomore year was upon us. The dance team met in the girls' restroom to get dressed and fix our hair for one last time. It was pretty crowded in there. I accidentally backed into Michaela.

"Oh, I'm sorry," I said instinctively, until I realized it was her. She just kind of looked at me blankly while the rest of the team paused, waiting to see what was going to happen next. We were all silent, and I don't think Michaela or myself even knew what was going to happen next. There was a long, awkward silence. We just stared at each other, uncomfortably.

"Come on you two. Give it a rest," my friend Tabitha said, being brave enough to break the silence. "You guys are friends. Now say you're sorry, give each other a hug, and put an end to this nonsense already."

Almost simultaneously, we obeyed. It was like a weight had been lifted, not only off of the two of us, but the whole dance team as well. There was practically an audible sigh of relief among all of us. Everything, after months of hating, girl drama and negativity was put to rest. We both wanted this. I think we both wanted this for a long time. We were mentally exhausted from keeping up this charade. If this had been a Netflix series, I am pretty sure the entire dance team would have clapped and we would break into song just like in High School Musical.

From there, we went onto the basketball court during halftime in front of a standing room only crowd. We danced our butts off to "Mountain Music" by Alabama while the entire crowd was on their feet. You could hear them hootin' and hollerin' and having themselves a grand old time. Hands were clapping and feet were stomping. When we got to our dramatic ending, we received a standing O. It was the best night of my sophomore year.

The rest of the year went pretty smoothly. Michaela and I weren't the same. We would say hi to each other in the hallway. We'd make eye contact and smile. She didn't get her friends after me although, they still didn't really like me. They weren't pushing me anymore or saying anything to me, but they would roll their eyes at Michaela and me in disagreement whenever we would exchange small pleasantries with each other. School finally became a much safer place for me. This I could handle.

Chapter 5: Magic

"Just a little bit of magic pulls me through…"

Summer came and Viv was still wrapped up in Terrence. We'd hang out on occasion. Viv and I had an understanding. We were more like sisters than friends. I knew she was always going to be there for me, even if we didn't hang out all the time. I was never jealous (well, maybe just a little) of her relationship with Terrence. As cheesy as it was, it was kind of dreamy. Viv was never caught up in any drama either. Her and Terrence had promised each other that they were not going to drink. They were very "goody goody", as Charlie would always say about me, but they never seemed to be in the kind of trouble I was always in. They both went to church together too. I went to some of her church's youth events from time to time. It was always fun, but I never had a real desire to attend church every Sunday. Viv was solid. She was my foundation and my role model at the end of the day.

I got a summer job at Cedar Point, which was a popular amusement park about thirty minutes from my house. I took photos of guests at the front gate as they entered. Once the photos developed, a crew which included myself, would assemble the photos into keychains. It was a terrible job, but we would get a commission! Yes, that's right, at age 15, I was making a commission! After we would take 5 rolls of photos, we would get a quarter for each roll after that.

You couldn't come in from the hot sun into our little air conditioned booth until you took at least 5 rolls of film. This was not easy. I would be out there from 9am to sometimes 2pm sweating to death. Once I went into the restroom to splash my face with cold water. When I came out, some of the customers were sympathetic to me because I looked so ungodly hot. They let me take a ton of photos. Another time I fake hyperventilated so that the miniature park ambulance would come and get me. Dramatic, I know, but literally there was no relief from the hot Sandusky sun. There was no shade. I knew if I did some kind of theatrical performance I would buy myself a free ticket to the air conditioned first aid station. People either wanted all kinds of photos or they hated us for trying to stop them for a quick photo. If they only knew how much it would help if they would just stop for one second for a photo. They didn't even have to buy it. Eventually I got smarter with my photographing tactics. If it was a family, I would take a close up and a far away shot of the whole family, then just the kids, then just the parents. I would get 6 photos out of that. Oh, and what's that? Oh, your child blinked, I need to take it again. Parents would happily oblige. If it was a group of teenagers, I would take enough close ups and far away shots so each person in the group could have their own keychains. Then I would take close ups and far away shots of each couple. Then just the guys. Then just the girls. You're looking at about 40 shots with just one willing group of teenagers. It was genius!

As agonizing as it was, Cedar Point had its benefits. Here, I was somehow likable. No one ever made fun of my eyes or told me to go back to my own country. I met kids from other schools. It was like I had a clean slate. I was not Reverend Mother, or The Weird Asian girl. No one thought I was a goody goody or prude. I was just simply me, and I discovered that here, people other than Viv, liked me. Because working as a Cedar Point photographer was so excruciating, it was easy to bond with the rest of the staff. It seems when people have to go through some kind of hardship together, they bond. It was hot, we barely made anything, customers would yell at us, but at the end of the day, we had each other.

I met my friend Amy at Cedar Point. Coincidentally, she lived in Amherst and I lived in Amherst as well, but the south side, so in other words, South Amherst. We really hit it off. She was kind and funny and a little older than me, by just a year, but she seemed wise beyond her years. She had the coolest clothes, and her nails were always perfect. She would go to the salon every other week to get her nails filled. She knew how to dress, and had a car and a job. She was super sentimental, relatable and responsible. It seemed like she understood me right from the start. Eventually she drove me to work instead of my mom. It was awesome. We'd listen to the best music, and have really meaningful conversations. We started hanging out all the time.

After work one night, we went to this really dive teen club called the Putt 'n Club. It was in an old barn (of course) about five minutes from where I lived. It had a jukebox, a pool table, a concession stand and a few small tables. Neon Rainbow as well as many other Alan Jackson hits would be playing on the jukebox. We would just hang around there and shoot pool together. After not much was going on, two guys walked in. They were both average height. One was somewhat overweight, yet stocky. He probably was on the football team, I assumed. The other guy? Well, I was kind of smitten. He had blue eyes, wavy, light brown hair, and they both dressed pretty stylish. Not the flannels and work boots that I was used to. These two were clean cut. What really made them noticeable to me was that they walked in with a ton of confidence. They walked in like they owned the place. They had a vibe about them that I could not explain.

"Hey Nate!" Amy said with enthusiasm.

Wait. Amy actually knows these two very overly confident guys? What the...?

"Cyndi, this is my brother Nate and our cousin Matt."

Ahhh....very interesting, I thought. These two looked like money and a ton of fun. They bought themselves each a can of pop and set them on the ledge next to the pool table. I really stunk at the game of pool, but I don't think anyone was really all that interested in the game itself. It was just something social to do in order to pass the time.

After some small talk and Amy and I getting beaten several times, we walked out into the parking lot. Nate and Matt each lit up a cigarette. Amy and I leaned up against her car. The night air was comfortably cool for June.

"You wanna hear some Helen Keller jokes?" Nate asked.

"Sure!" we said.

"How did Helen Keller's parents punish her?" Nate asked and paused.

"How?" we said, in unison.

"They would rearrange the furniture!"

Amy and I laughed and laughed, and we might burn in hell for doing so, but it was funny, and that was only the beginning. It was the early 90's and we were young. People didn't get as offended as they do today. They were just jokes.

"How did Helen Keller burn her hands?" Matt asked.

"How?" we said in unison again.

"By reading the waffle iron!" he said, cracking himself up.

"Did you know Helen Keller had a dog?" Nate asked.

"No." I said, waiting for the punchline.

"Neither did she!" he said, barely able to contain himself.

We went on like this for about an hour. I'm pretty sure Nate and Matt had put on this performance several times in the past. They were well rehearsed. I never laughed that much in my life. My face was hurting.

After this night, I got to know not only Amy's brother and cousin, but I also met her other cousin Charlene and a few other of their friends from a neighboring school that they knew, Jay and Emmet. They were all better looking than any guy I had seen at my school. Most importantly, they didn't think I was strange looking either. If anything, I think they found me a tiny bit attractive which was something I had never known before.

I had a pool, so everyone started gathering at my house. I think this made my parents very happy because I was always home and they got to know my friends. For my birthday, Amy brought over Nate and Matt, who brought with them Emmet and Jay. My friend Samson even started tagging along and he brought his friend, Rex. Charlene decided to come over for my birthday. Viv too, without Terrence even! There were so many cars in my driveway that some of them had to park in the grass! All I could do was step back and take it all in. These people were here for me. It felt really great!

We decided to pack ourselves into 2 cars and drove to this other club called Johnny T's out by Cedar Point. It was much bigger and a little more prestigious than the Putt 'n Club. This place had a bowling alley, a restaurant AND pool tables. Lots of them.

We did everything. We ate lots of bar food, played pool and went bowling. It was my 16th birthday and I felt more than special. Little by little, life was starting to turn around. I never felt attractive at my school. I was always anxious to go to school fearing that someone would definitely make me feel less than human. But with these new friends, I had nothing to fear.

Amy spent the night after all of the fun and festivities. She left in the morning, before even eating anything for breakfast. I sat at the table and poured myself some Kellog's Frosted Mini Wheats and a glass of ice water. It was what I ate every morning for years. I was a very picky eater. I hadn't even tried a Big Mac in all of my 16 years! I turned on the Saturday Morning Cartoons. The Smurfs were on, which, although I was a teenager, never got old. I started slurping up my cereal. My mom sat down and joined me.

"Michaela stopped by yesterday," she said.

Odd, I thought. Although we made up, she never came over. We hadn't hung out together since the cafeteria debacle.

"Well, that's weird. What did she want?" I asked, genuinely curious.

"She was wondering why there were so many cars here and if they were all friends of yours. She also hinted at wanting to be invited over to hang out with you. I told her where you were. She said she would stop over later today."

Huh. Baffling.

"She stayed here for about an hour and we just talked."

Huh again. This is all so random. My mom didn't give much detail about what they talked about, but it did seem like my mom wanted me to be friends with her again. I kind of felt bad. I mean, we were very close at one time. Now I met these other cool friends all at once. Had I not met them, maybe I would have thought about hooking up with Michaela again.

She came over the next day, just like she said she would. It was early afternoon, and I was still kind of groggy from the night before. There she was, standing at my screen door as I happened to walk by.

"Hey!" she said. "Mind if I come in?"

"Of course! Come on in!'" I said as I led her to the kitchen. "How have you been?"

"Well, Scott and I hang out a lot. He lives down the street from you, so I pass your house every day. I thought I'd stop by."

This made sense.

"I also needed to tell you something," she became very serious. Although we had not been normal lately, I had never known her to be serious. She's going to tell me she's pregnant, I thought. I know she is.

"What? What is it? You're pregnant? What?" I said nervously.

"Uhhh, no. That's not it."

"Then what?"

"I uh, I tried to kill myself the other night."

My heart broke in two, right there, in my body, as I heard her words.

"You what? Why?"

"I don't know. Scott and I got into an argument. It was stupid," she said.

"How? What did you try to do?"

"Gun fluid," she said. "I drank it. Scott found me and took me to the ER. They pumped my stomach and well, here I am!" she said, half nonchalantly and half serious.

This was not the news I was expecting to hear. Why was she telling me this? This was absolutely insane. I grabbed her shoulders and got real close to her face.

"Look, I am sorry for all that we went through. I am glad you are here. You cannot ever do this again. We are still going to go to college together. I am still going to marry Dylan from 90210. We are still going to live in California. I do not want to lose you again. Do you understand?" I was shaking her. I think I was scaring her. Tears started to form in my eyes and hers.

"I've missed you. We have so much more to do together. We really need to make up for lost time, you know?" I said.

"We do. I won't do this again. It was really dumb" she said, looking down. "Tell you what, when is your next day off?"

"Wednesday of next week. Why?"

"Let's go to Cedar Point. Scott will bring a friend. It'll be fun."

"Okay, that sounds perfect!"

From there, we moved to my room. I sat on my bed while she stood, looking at her hair in the mirror.

"What do you think about my hair? I don't think it's long enough," she said. She had her neck tilted way back, in effort to make her hair appear to seem longer. I never understood why she fussed over herself so much. She had natural wavy hair and sparkling blue eyes. She was thin and gorgeous with a killer personality. She was that kind of person where, when she walked in a room, you knew she was there. You could tell by her carefree laugh. She was never serious. She lived a totally carefree life that was all about fun. It was comforting, knowing we were going to start the summer off hanging out again. It was her last summer before she was going to be a senior.

"Geez, Michaela. You are gorgeous," I said, kind of envious of her. "Everyone loves you."

We spent the rest of the afternoon just catching up. I told her how excited I was to get to take my driver's license test soon. She told me about Scott, and I told her about Matt, Nate, Amy and Charlene. It was like nothing had ever happened. We just picked up right where we left off.

Chapter 6: It's All I Can Do

"It's all I can do to keep waiting for you…"

Later that evening after Michaeala left, my phone rang, you know, the cool Swatch phone. It was Charlene.

"Hey.Wednesday, a bunch of us are getting together at Nate's house. His parents will be out of town. You gotta come. I think my cousin Matt is really into you," Charlene said.

"You're kidding, right?" I said.

No guy as cute as Matt had ever shown any interest in me at all.

"No seriously. I think he likes you. You have to come!" she said.

"I was supposed to go to Cedar Point with Michaela, but I am pretty sure she will understand. Let me talk to her."

"Isn't she the girl who you got in a fight with in the cafeteria? You two are friends again?" she asked. Charlene went to a different school and didn't know all the details.

"Well, yeah. Actually, we made up before school let out. The fight is water under the bridge," I explained. "I'm sure she will understand. I told her all about Matt! She would be excited for me!"

Of course she understood. She also told me that her friend Kristina and her boyfriend were going to go to Cedar

Point too, so I think that kind of took the edge off of me not going. Plus, Kristina was one of the girls who did most of the shoving back in the days when we were hating each other. Once I knew she was going, I really didn't want to go. Since she and Michaela had been hanging out together this entire time, it was best I didn't go. I would have been the 5th wheel anyway, riding all the rides by myself like a dork. It all worked out.

My mom loved Amy, so it was no big deal for me to go there, trusting that we would be supervised. I don't know how I ever managed to meet kids whose parents never caught them doing anything wrong. I got caught doing everything. In 8th grade, Felicia and I decided to sneak out in the middle of the night to hang out with her neighbor boys across the street. It was -13 below zero and we were really stupid. We ransacked her brothers' bedroom for layers of clothes and out the door we went. Her mom decided to check on us in the middle of the night and saw the boys' room all a wreck. She thought for sure a stranger came into the house and took us or something, so she called my parents and the police.

There was only one policeman in our tiny 1 stoplight town. He never found us. In fact, we beat him plus our parents back to the house. I remember Felicia and I frantically pulling off our layers to climb into bed in effort to fool our parents into thinking that we were really in bed all along. Yeah, that was going to work!

Of course it didn't! Once my dad arrived and figured out I was fine, he pulled me down the stairs by my hair and grounded me for 2 months! Once that grounding was served, I went out with some of my friends (Viv was not there, for the record), and got into a car with some 18 year old boys who gave us beer. We got caught and were taken to the police station. One of the boys took off, but the other one had to take the heat. He even ended up going to court for giving beer to minors. Back then, you could buy beer when you were 18. It's probably best that the law has since changed to age 21. Anyway, I got caught doing that too. My parents had to pick me up from the police station. It was awful, and needless to say, I got grounded again, this time for 3 months. If you do the math, I was grounded for 5 out of the 9 months of my 8th grade school year. I should have just stuck with Viv. I never got into any kind of trouble with her. When left to my own devices, I almost always got caught.

Nate and Amy had older friends who picked up a ton of alcohol. Charlene had somehow scored a 2 liter of Sun Country, one for her and one for myself. My only other experience with drinking was with Charlie, and we all know how that turned out.

Charlene and I drank right out of the bottle all night long. It tasted like kool aid, but like carbonated kool aid. It was very easy to drink it fast without really realizing it. We stumbled around the house with our arms around each other all night long, being carefree and laughing at nothing. She introduced me to all of her friends from her school. The song "Have A Drink on Me" by ACDC was playing loudly on the stereo. Charlene and I were already pretty happy, if you know what I mean. She climbed up onto the kitchen table and pulled me up beside her. I guess it was tradition at her school to drink straight through the chorus. Whenever the lead singer of ACDC sang, "Have a drink on me," the room got silent because everyone in the room took a swig. Char and I continued to dance and sing at the top of our lungs like two fools.

Suddenly, the phone rang.

"EVERYONE, SHUT UP! IT'S PROBABLY MY PARENTS!" Nate shouted. And just like that, the stereo was silenced, everyone got quiet and still. You could hear a pin drop.

"Yes, Ma. Everything's fine. Matt and I are playing video games and Cyndi and Amy are in Amy's room. Don't worry," he said, smirking at all of us as we listened in silently. "Okay. Okay. I will.Bye," he said, and hung up the phone.

"Everything's cool!" he said. Just as quickly as we all got silent, the stereo was back on, Charlene and I got back to our table top dancing and singing performance. A crowd had gathered around us to watch and cheer us on.

"Who threw eggs into the microwave?" Amy shouted with disgust. She ran off with Nate and the two of them proceeded to clean it up the best that they could. Charlene and I climbed down off the table. She passed out on the couch and I flopped down next to her. I looked to my left and there was Matt, cool as a cucumber. He had a beer in one hand and his elbows were propped up confidently on the top of the couch.

"How's it going? You and Charlene seem to be hitting it off," Matt said.

"Yeah, she's a lot of fun to party with," I said. "I feel like we have known each other for a long time.

"She's pretty crazy. Especially when she's been drinking. You gotta watch that one!" he said, chuckling.

"I liked your Helen Keller jokes the other night. I might burn in hell for laughing," I said, not really knowing what else to say.

"Yeah, it's just all fun. That's all. No big deal," he said. "Listen.I was wondering if you'd want to go out sometime? Our football team has a scrimmage coming up soon, and Nate plays. You want to go and watch him with me?"

Oh my gosh! Was this really happening? Stay calm. I begged myself.

"Sure! That sounds like fun. Here's my number," I said and wrote it on a receipt that was sitting on the end table beside me. Out of nowhere, I heard a hacking sound. It was Charlene. She was waking up and vomiting all over the floor.

"C'mon, Char!" Matt said, a little annoyed, but started to pick her up anyway. I held her hair back as he walked her to the bathroom. He propped her up over the toilet while I sat behind her, still holding her hair.

"I'm going to see what I can do about the carpet. Amy is going to kill her," he said.

"Okay. I'll stay here with her," I said.

Once it seemed as if Charlene was finished, I moved her into Amy's room to sleep it off.

Amy, who was pretty responsible, somehow managed to take me home that night. I wasn't feeling the greatest, so I was thankful that she did. My parents were both asleep, so I quietly crept into my room, and changed into my pjs, feeling a little too tipsy to make it into the shower. Amy needed to get back to her house to clean up any evidence before her parents got home. I was in no condition to be helpful.

What a great night, I thought to myself. I looked at the clock. Dean would be calling soon. We had a routine of talking every Saturday night without fail. It was nice to have a friend who was a guy and didn't go to my school. He wasn't aware of the dork I really was. I picked up the phone and started dialing the time and temperature number: 246-1234...I only had to dial it 2 times before I heard the beep of the call waiting. Sure enough it was Dean.

"Hey," he said. "What'd you do tonight?"

"I had the best night. I went to my friend Amy's party. It was a blast, but then my friend Charlene threw up all over the carpet, so that kind of stunk, literally," I laughed at my own pun.

I told Dean all about Matt asking me out. Dean and I were never more than friends, so it wasn't weird for me to be telling him this. He was a little protective about it, but in more of a brotherly kind of way. I also told him about how Michaela had stopped over last week and how happy I was that we were friends again.

Soon enough, it was 1am.

"Oh my goodness, Dean! It is already 1am! I am going to sit by the window. Now that Michaela and I have been talking, she honks her horn on her way back from her boyfriend's house. She must have to be home around 1am because it has been right about now, every night, that she stops in front of my house and wails on the horn. Shhhh....she should be driving by soon," I said excitedly.

It was a cool crisp night in mid-August. The air felt refreshing on my face. I loved the scent of the evening outdoor air. It was pretty quiet. At most I could hear the crickets, and oddly, an owl would hoot every now and again. I remember when I was little I would hear it and it would terrify me like everything else did, especially at night. I would always yell for my mom to sleep with me. I was such a scaredy cat.

You would think the silence between Dean and I would be uncomfortable, but it wasn't. I think he, too, wanted to hear Michaela's horn beep. We sat for a few moments and waited.

"I hear a car coming. I bet it's her. I'll hold the phone up against the screen for you," I said hopefully.

The car rushed by and all we heard was crickets once again.

"Hmmm…that's odd," I said. "She will do it. I swear she will! Just wait." We waited as long as two very talkative teenagers could wait, which wasn't long.

"Do you have FFA at your school?" I asked, randomly, breaking the silence.

"Uhhhh, no. What does that stand for?" he asked.

"It stands for Future Farmers of America," I said.

All I could hear on the other end was total and complete laughter. Not just a chuckle but an all out belly laugh that left Dean gasping for air, he was laughing so hard.

"I don't get it. What's so funny about that?"

No answer, just more laughing. I waited and I waited. After what felt like forever, he finally calmed down.

"And what does one do in the FFA? Enlighten me please!" he said, chuckling.

"Well, if you must know, we have this special day at school. It's called FFA Day. If you have a farm tractor or lawn mower, you get to drive it to school that day. Then there's a hay tossing contest among other things. Maybe a pig calling contest? I can't remember all the details, but it's pretty fun!"

More laughter. I almost hung up. I waited and waited as he continued to poke fun at my school.

2:00AM rolled around. We had been talking for almost 2 hours. I didn't even realize it.

"Well, I guess I'm going to go," I said, still perched up on the headboard of my bed, almost forgetting why I was sitting there. "I guess Michaela isn't going to drive by tonight. Or maybe she did and we missed it because you were laughing so hard, loser," I said jokingly.

"Blah, blah," he said. "Hearing you talk about FFA is way more entertaining than waiting to hear Michaela's stupid horn. Goodnight."

"Goodnight," I said. I closed my window and went to sleep.

Chapter 7: You're All I've Got Tonight

"I need you..."

Ring! Ring!

Apparently I fell asleep with the phone right next to me. It ripped me out of my deep slumber.

"Hello?" I said, sleepily?

"It's Viv," she sounded super serious.

"What time is it?" I asked, a little annoyed. I wonder if this is what a hangover might feel like?

"7:30am. Listen..."

"WHAT? Why are you calling me so early?" I said impatiently.

"Because, something happened," she paused. "Michaela died," she said.

"WHAT? How? You can't be serious. This is not funny," I said, sitting straight up in my bed.

"Look, I wouldn't joke about this. It was just on the news. She was in a car accident very early this morning, like around 1am."

Suddenly everything was spinning. My heart felt like it was going to explode right out of my chest. I don't know what I said, but I started screaming and screaming. I was losing all control of my emotions.

"I'm coming over," Viv said.

My mom came tearing into my room. She was saying something to me, but I was not comprehending. I was standing up, clutching my sheets, anything that I could grab onto because I felt like I might be falling. Maybe this is what falling apart feels like. My mom was grabbing me and holding me up, trying to figure out what happened. Then the doorbell rang.

"VIV! YOU TELL ME RIGHT NOW THAT THIS ISN'T TRUE. RIGHT NOW! SAY IT!" I said as I was running towards the screen door.

She just stood there staring at me. Silent.

We were standing on my front porch. It was a gorgeous August morning. The birds were chirping. Cars were casually going by. The world was still spinning while mine came to a screeching halt.

I collapsed. Viv did her best to hold on to me but somehow I slid down her whole body and was laying at her feet, still holding my pillow and the sheets I had ripped off my bed. I was falling and falling into the earth. No amount of my strength was keeping me up. I was grasping at anything. Viv's legs. The sheets. The blankets. Anything to make me stop falling. I noticed I was actually on the ground. Why couldn't I get any closer to it? Why was I falling?

"Nooooo, nooooo," was all I could say that made any sense to anyone that heard my shrieks. Everything else was just plain screaming nonsense.

The last thing I remember was Viv holding me. My soaking wet face was dripping onto her bare thigh. There were so many tears that I could see a small puddle forming on the cement of my front porch. My hair was sticking to my face. I could taste the salt of my own tears. My body lay in a fetal position while Viv sat silently, stroking my back. There was nothing she could say. All she could do was sit and listen to my cries until I was empty.

Even though I physically had no more tears to cry, I was still hyperventilating. I wasn't trying to speak, but it was just that unexpected, unrhythmic and uncontrollable breathing that my body was doing all on its own. As I kept forcing myself to take deep breaths, I started to calm down a little.

"My mom and I are going to go to Michaela's house to check on her mom," Viv said. "You should come with us."

Go? To her house? Like, with all of her things everywhere? I was feeling emotions that I had never felt before.

Apparently I had a few tears left because as I was thinking over Viv's request, a few slowly fell from my eyes and down my cheeks.

"Oh, I don't know if I can do that," I said.

"If you feel like this, how do you think her mother feels?" she asked.

I sat a little longer, still on my front porch, the cement cold on my skin. I was breathing normally now, but the tears were still streaming and my pj shirt was getting wet. I nodded my head.

"Okay. You're right. I should go."

I threw on a pair of jeans shorts and the first t-shirt I could find. I ran a brush through my hair and brushed my teeth. Viv threw her arm around my shoulder as we wearily walked down the street to her house.

Her mom was already waiting in the car, that Crown Vic, where Viv and I would belt out tunes after school when things were easy. Being in the car on this day felt strange and heavy. I pulled my seatbelt on and stared out the window. We were all quiet, no radio to fill the space, yet it did not feel awkward.

Michaela's driveway was long and surrounded by trees that made it look like a small forest in the front of her house. Viv's mom drove us slowly up the drive. To my right was the picnic table where Dean and I talked for hours months ago. To the left was where Michaela and I were walking up to her house one night, and her friend Jean snuck up behind us and scared us half to death. In front of me was the front door to the house where Michaela was normally the one to greet me when I would come over to hang out. Then, off to the side, I saw where she usually parked her little red Fiero. It wasn't there, and I knew she wasn't either, but I could sense her all around me.

We knocked on the door and there was her mother, looking suddenly older than her age. I opened the door so I could get to her and she collapsed into my arms, very much how I had when Viv came to my door just an hour or so earlier. This time, I had to be the strong one.

If you ever heard the sound of a mother crying over her dead child, it's indescribable. I have no words to describe the agony of this sound. I pray that I never have to hear this sound again. She was squeezing me so tightly, and I was surprised at her strength and how much she needed me at this moment. Adults don't *need* kids, or do they? Maybe their own kids, but me? She was relying on me to keep her standing. I felt like I was holding all of her pieces together.

"Can you tell me what happened?" I asked, not crying shockingly. It is amazing how the body and soul sense when it is not a good time to cry, but to be strong for someone else.

We sat down on the couch. I looked around. There was where we threw all the beer cans after her party. This was the couch I was sitting on when I encountered the boy who had condoms under his hat. I held her hand in mine.

"She went to Cedar Point last night with Scott and another couple. She was tired, and she should not have driven home," she said, speaking slowly, but kind of in a trance and staring off into space.

"I think she fell asleep at the wheel. That's what the police said anyway. Her car went off the road and… and…" she was starting to not be able to breathe like I did.

"It's okay," I said. "Take your time."

She nodded and took a deep breath. "Her car went off the road," she repeated, "And she hit a telephone pole. Her.her sunroof…" she paused. The three of us just waited patiently.

"Her…her sunroof was open…and…and when she hit the pole, her car flipped," she said, shaking her head. I thought she was done, but she wasn't.

"When the car flipped, she flew out of the sunroof and…and…" We waited some more.

"She wasn't wearing her seatbelt. She flew out and the car, it…it…" she was squeezing my hand so tightly. "It rolled on top of her. There was head trauma, they said."

I wanted to vomit. I didn't want to picture this. But now, it was out there, and I could not unsee it in my mind.

"Poor Scott insisted on going to the hospital with me to identify her body," she cried. "His mother didn't want him to go, but he hopped in the car with me and no one could stop him."

Her body? This can't be real. She's a person, not a body. In her mom's other hand was a picture.

"Look at this. This was taken last week at a barbecue at my sister's house." She was gripping it tightly.

I looked, and there she was, alive and happy, that smile that lit up the room, those blue eyes and long curly lashes that could talk any high school boy into getting her way. Her sandy blond hair with natural waves. My mind flashed back to just last week when she was looking at her hair in my mirror, wishing it was longer. I could see it like it just happened. She cocked her head back so her hair would look longer as she twisted around to see the back of it in my mirror. She would never do that again. She will never be standing in my room again. She was just there. How can this be?

Viv's mom took Michaela's mom into the kitchen to talk about probably the next steps, I assumed. Viv sat next to me holding my hand.

All I could do was observe. Her sweat jacket was hanging on the hook by the door. The wipe off board in the hall by the kitchen said, "Mich, defrost the meat for dinner. Don't forget, Mom." Her shoes sat on the floor innocently waiting for her to return by the door under her sweat jacket.

"Okay girls. We have some things to take care of," Viv's mom said, interrupting my thoughts in her normal cheery voice.

"You going to be okay?" I asked her mom.

"No, she said. "I will never be okay."

I nodded my head. I understood, because I probably would never be okay either.

I wasn't sure where Viv's mom was taking us and I didn't ask. Nothing really mattered at the moment. I knew she needed to handle something for Michaela's mom. Probably some grown up type stuff. We drove in silence again.

I noticed that wherever we were going, we were retracing the route Michaela would have taken to get home from Scott's house. We pulled out of her driveway and drove north. We turned right onto Viv and my street. We passed Viv's house and then mine. We drove about 5 minutes more past my house and then I saw it: the accident scene.

The road curves around to the right and then to the left then straight for a few yards. There was caution tape all around the scene. Someone's house was set back about 50 yards. I could see her tire tracks etched in the mud going through the ditch by the road and then off into the yard. The earth was gouged out of the ground.

We were driving about 35 mph around the curve in the road, so there wasn't time to take it all in. I'm not sure that I wanted or needed to. The few seconds it took us to drive by was enough to scar my 16 year old brain for life. I saw the ditch, the mud and the house all kind of in a blur yet unforgettable all at once. It was the telephone pole that got me.

It was tilted over at the center like it would snap any second. The cables at the top were probably keeping it from falling completely over, so it was hanging, but not broken in half quite yet. There was a chunk missing from the telephone pole. For a moment pain ran through my body as if to sympathize with what Michaela's body must have gone through.

All of this went by in a flash, but it felt like it was going in slow motion for me. Right in front of me were the last moments of my friend's life. A million questions ran through my mind. Was she tired? Did she fall asleep? Was it wet? Did she lose control of the car? Had it been raining? I don't think so. Could she have taken the curve in the road too quickly? But wait. The road is straight where she went off the road. What happened to you, Michaela? Did you try to do the unthinkable? The thing you promised me you would never do? Did you do this on purpose? Was I the only one that knew? Was this my fault? Why didn't I tell anyone? Could I have prevented this? My head was spinning and my voice was shrieking once again. I knew sound must have been coming out of my mouth as I turned to see the scene just a moment longer out the back window as we drove by. All Viv could do was put her arm around me. There were no words that could have made this moment any better. None.

The rest of the day was a blur. We ran some errands, but I don't know what they were. I know I went along, but I don't know where we went. Somehow I had made it back into my own bed. It must have been the afternoon because the sun was still out, which was baffling to me. How in the world could the day be so cheery when I was in the darkest place I had ever been?

Then it dawned on me. *Oh my gosh. Dean. He probably doesn't know.* I dialed the phone.

Keep in mind, Dean and I only spoke to each other on the phone at night and mostly on the weekends, so it was completely out of character for me to call him in the middle of the day.

"Hello?" he said, unsuspectingly.

"Hey. It's me," my voice wavered.

"Oh hey, what's up? You never call me at this hour. You okay?" he asked.

"Not really. I found out why Michaela didn't beep her horn last night," I said solemnly.

"What are you talking about?" he asked. Sometimes guys are so dumb. It was such a minor detail last night, but now I realized it had been the foreshadowing moment to what I was about to tell him.

"Oh my gosh, do you listen to anything I say?" I said, getting annoyed and my voice cracking.

"C'mon. What are you trying to tell me? Yeah, okay, I remember, you were waiting for her to drive by last night, you nerd. What's the big deal? She probably forgot," he said.

"No, she didn't forget. She didn't!" I was getting worked up all over again. When will I run out of energy? "She died, Dean. She's dead. She's dead…" I screamed.

"You are a nut job," he said. "She's probably sitting right there next to you. You guys are ridiculous, you know that? This is stupid. I can hear her laughing."

"She's not here, I swear. I wouldn't joke about this. I don't know what you are hearing, but it isn't her."

"I don't believe you," he said.

"Fine. Don't," I said. "Check the newspaper. I'll see you at the funeral."

"You two are sick," he said, and he hung up the phone.

Chapter 8: Moving In Stereo

"It's so tough to get up..."

Between the day that I found out and the funeral, I became a basket case.

"I was supposed to be with her, Viv," I said, in a trance. We were sitting in my room.

"What are you talking about?" she asked.

"I was supposed to go to Cedar Point with her, but I didn't. Nate and Amy had a party that night and Matt was going to be there. You know, Matt? Amy and Charlene's cousin? Charlene said he wanted to ask me out, so I didn't want to miss out on that opportunity. And Kristina and her boyfriend ended up going with Scott and Michaela to Cedar Point. Kristina still hates me, I think, from back when Michaela and I weren't getting along, so I didn't want to go anyway and Mich totally understood. There would have been 5 of us, and I would have been the 5th wheel and would have had to ride everything alone. So, I didn't go."

Viv nodded. She was always pretty good at just letting me talk. She should be a counselor or something.

"Viv, I could have prevented this."

"How?" she asked.

"Well, if I would have gone with Michaela, I would have driven back with her and she would not have fallen asleep. We would have turned up the radio or would have been talking or something. Anything! She would not have fallen asleep if I was with her!"

"Or?" Viv asked, in a counselor kind of way, letting me process all of this on my own.

"Or what?" I said, clueless.

"Or, you would have been in the accident too," she said calmly.

I had not thought of that. Wow. That one decision. That one tiny little decision to go to Nate and Amy's party saved my life, possibly, or was it the reason why Michaela lost hers?

"Tell me this. Why do I get to be here and she doesn't?" I asked.

"I don't know, sweetie," Viv replied. "I don't know. All I can think of is that your work is not done."

"What do you mean?"

"You have more work to do. God's work. I don't know what that is, but your time isn't up yet," she explained.

Viv and Terrence went to church every Sunday. They didn't drink. They didn't lie to their parents. They were nauseating. They were the couple all parents would want their teenagers to be. All they ever did was hang out at each other's houses and hold each other or watch TV. They never went to parties. I, on the other hand, never went to church. We might have gone on an occasional Easter Sunday or something, but I knew nothing about God. In fact, I had a bone to pick with Him right now.

"Why did He take her? Why? She's so young and WE had work to do. We had college to do and more parties and traveling to do. Why her? Why now?" Tears were running down my face again, but at least I wasn't hyperventilating anymore like the day before.

"I'm not sure that he *took* her. I'm pretty sure God's as broken up about it as you are," she explained.

"This makes no sense. I thought God was all controlling and all knowing and all of that. I don't understand."

"I don't think you are supposed to understand. But God also gives us free will. See, she didn't have to get into the car and drive, especially if she was tired. You don't know. Maybe God tried to stop her. Maybe she thought about putting her seatbelt on but was rushing. You just don't know. You'll probably never know. You are just going to have to accept that."

"The thing is, I have free will too, right? And if that is the case, then I chose not to go with her. I chose to try to get a date with Matt. If I would have chosen to go with her, then I could have kept her awake," I said.

"Or, you wouldn't be here now. And then what would I do?"

"Well, I guess you wouldn't be having this conversation with me."

"The thing is, this is how it played out. And it's okay to be sad and mad. You should probably talk to God about all of this," she said.

"Well, blah," I said, frustrated. I had never talked to God. I might have asked Him for a puppy when I was little and I never got one for years after that. What would I say anyway?

"All I am saying is that all of this is horrible. If nothing else, try talking to God. Just try. You starting a relationship with Him might be the best thing that comes out of this. What do you have to lose? So, hey, I gotta get going. I'm supposed to hang out with Terrence tonight."

"Really? Can't you just stay here?" I begged, a little annoyed.

"Well, how about this. I'll go meet up with him for a bit and then I'll come back and just stay the night. Sound good?"

"Yeah, I suppose. I just don't want to be alone tonight. I feel empty and scared for some reason. Just hurry back. I don't know what to do with myself." Out the door she went to walk back to her house.

There I sat, all alone in my room, looking at the exact spot where Michaela stood just about a week ago, complaining about her hair, replaying it in my mind, over and over. It was pretty quiet in my room. I could hear my parents watching TV in the next room. Oddly, I could feel a presence all around me. I can't explain it, but it was a strange feeling. It made me anxious and afraid. Then it dawned on me. Viv's not coming back. Not ever.

Chapter 9: Hello Again

"The journey ends, you tied your knots
You made your friends, you left the scene
Without a trace..."

I leapt out of my bed wearing a pair of boxers and one of my dad's old t-shirts. I tore out the door in a panic. I could hear my mom ask where I was going, but I didn't answer and she let it go, assuming I was headed to Viv's. The screen door slammed behind me.

It was a little bit cooler on this mid August evening. The sun was starting to go down, but it was still pretty bright out considering it had to be around 8pm. My bare feet pounded on the ground. I could feel each step vibrate through my bones as I took off down the street, but I was numb and felt no pain. I was headed to Viv's. As I rounded the corner into her driveway, she was just pulling out in her mom's beige Crown Vic.

"WAIT!" I screamed in a panic. Viv slammed the car in park and quickly got out of the car.

Tears were streaming down my face as I threw my arms around her neck. Startled, she just stood there patting my back gently, not sure what she should do.

"What? What is it?," she asked, concerned.

"You can't go. You can't get in the car. You just can't go."

"What are you talking about?" she asked.

"Because…", I pulled away from her, wiping the tears from my face as I rocked my body back and forth with my arms folded. "Because you might not come back," I said, out of breath.

"Oh my gosh, Cyn! I'm going to come back," she said.

"You might not. How can you be so sure?" I whined, almost sounding like a baby. Wow, it must be awful to be a baby. Babies can't possibly understand the concept of people coming and going.

She just stood there, looking at me, dumbfounded.

"Okay. Okay. I get it," she said, as she turned around to go into her house. I followed behind her, trying to catch my breath again from being so upset. She headed straight for the kitchen phone that hung on the wall and started dialing Terrence, I assumed. She opened up the back glass doors that went out to the patio that overlooked the woods. Then she closed it behind her causing the door to smash the cord and faced away from me. I guess she wanted some privacy.

I could see the back of her head nod occasionally while she spoke. I couldn't hear what she was saying. After a few minutes, I heard her open the door and she walked back inside. I heard her say, "Forever and always" before she hung up the phone. I rolled my eyes to myself.

You want to stay here or you want to walk down to your house?

The next few days were just kind of normal for everyone. I mean, what is one to do when they find out one of their friends has been killed? I just kind of aimlessly went about my business. Not necessarily thinking about Michaela, but not really thinking about anything.

When I was alone, it was like I could feel her in the room. You know, when someone actually is in the room, they must give off some sort of vibe. Like you might have your back turned and they walk in the room quietly. They might not say a word, but you know they are there. That was what it felt like when I was alone. There was a presence, but I felt scared and uneasy.

The day of Michaela's calling hours came. I wasn't sure how to react to it all since I had never been to one. I wasn't even sure what to wear, so I just put on the new outfit that my mom bought me for the first week of school: Black blazer with huge shoulder pads, a hot pink button down, long sleeved silky blouse and black gingham pattern pants. It was the early nineties. Don't judge. Huge shoulder pads were a thing.

When Viv and I arrived, there was a long line out the door. It was a sunny August afternoon. I always thought how odd it was that we had these gorgeous days when there had been a death. It just seems like in movies, when sad things happen, the weather seems to mirror the mood, you know? Real life is not the case. The earth just keeps doing it's thing, not really caring about the feelings of the rest of us.

We waited outside against the funeral home building located in my small town. There wasn't nearly enough parking. People young and old were waiting outside. Some people were already tearing up. I just felt a lump in my throat and a knot in my stomach. Every few minutes Viv and I were able to edge our way closer and closer to the entrance. When we finally reached the inside, it smelled strongly of flowers. Too strongly. I wonder, sick as it may be, do funeral homes encourage lots of flowers to cover up the smell of death? Because you could smell a hint of something else behind the strong floral scent.

Soft music was playing in the background. People were quietly talking among themselves. As we walked through, there were poster boards everywhere filled with photos. I wonder who put all that together. I can't imagine her mother could do it.

There were photos of her as a baby. So beautiful and innocent. Both of her parents were adoringly looking down at her, oblivious at the time of the photo, that this is how it is going to end. They had no idea that they would, 17 years later, see this photo hanging up on a poster board at a funeral home. It should be the other way around. This should have been a photo hanging on a poster board during her parents funeral perhaps. Isn't that how things are supposed to go? Parents first, children later?

There were more photos. Michaela as a toddler, then in grade school. All of her school photos were lined up in a row on a table, her baton, her pom poms and dance team uniform. It was almost like something you'd see at a graduation party. There were photos of us that I didn't even know she had. The one that caught my eye was the one where she was on my back doing a cheesy cheerleading pose in my bedroom. She had borrowed my white Forenza sweatshirt that had the brand name written in different colors vertically down the right side of the shirt. The funny thing about that sweatshirt was that it had a collar attached. It was navy blue. I have no idea what we were thinking in that photo, but somehow she must have managed to convince me to put my hands on my thighs and arch my back so she could hop on. She was laughing hysterically in the photo with her arms up in a V shape. I think she still has that sweatshirt of mine.

The line kept edging forward. Eventually we could see the open casket, but we were still too far to see it clearly. There was an elderly woman who was sitting in a chair next to the casket. She was trembling and her head was kind of rolling from side to side slowly, but rhythmic. She seemed as if in a trance, yet also very aware of where she was. It was heartbreaking and terrifying all at once to see.

I could see her mother at the front clinging to each visitor, audibly sobbing. My stomach knot was getting tighter and tighter with each step closer. *How am I supposed to act? What should I do?* I thought.

I got closer and soon I was right next to her grandmother. She was the one who was moving her head from side to side. I didn't recognize her until I was right next to her. It was uncomfortable and awkward. Do I hug her? Talk to her? I decided to just face forward. She was in no condition for physical contact or small talk. It felt like forever to be standing next to her like this.

From there, I started to see Michaela. I could see her sandy blond hair splayed out across the pillow that was propping up her head. I could see her face pointing towards the ceiling. I could start to make out her outfit.

Soon enough, her mother was in front of me. She looked me in the eyes, her eyes broken and full of sorrow. She put her hands on my shoulders, almost to try to stabilize herself and said, "She loved you" and then she clung to me again, like she had, days before when we went to her home. She clung to me longer than felt comfortable, but it only seemed long because I knew there were many many others who wanted to pay their respects one last time. When you are hugging a mother who has just lost her child suddenly, time doesn't matter. I don't even think anyone was irritated by it. Let the woman grieve for God's sake. I let her hold me as long as she needed. I didn't let go until she did. When she finally released me, she said, "Go. There she is."

I didn't want to look, but there I was, forced to. Viv slowly walked to the casket with me, a little bit ahead of me as if telling me with her movements that it's okay. I watched her stand there alone, shaking her head in silence, tears running down her face. After a moment, she looked at me as if to say, "It's your turn. You have to do this."

She put her hand out to me and I grabbed it tightly. When I got close, she put her arm around me while I shook with sobs. I put my head on her shoulder as my tears stained her white blouse.

I started with Michaela's face. This was not her. They painted over her eyelids with eyeliner. It wasn't smudged or anything. It was kind of like theater makeup. Her skin did not look real. It looked like if I touched it, my fingers would leave an imprint. Her face looked kind of flat as if gravity was pulling down on whatever they put on her face to give it shape. They drew on a smile. They took a lipliner and drew on a smile. Somehow they were able to shape her lips in such a way that she was smiling, but it was mostly drawn on. Not her real smile, not at all. Her hair was teased. She never teased her hair. It looked frizzy and wrong. She normally curled her bangs up with a few that would lay across her forehead. She normally had natural curls that seemed playful. Not like this. This was not her.

I immediately recognized her outfit. Her mother bought it for her for her senior pictures. She had those taken just a few weeks ago. It was a hot pink button down, short sleeve, silky feeling shirt, similar to what I had on. She had on aqua blue shorts of the same material that had suspenders that went up and over her shoulders. The suspenders buttoned at her waist.

The way she was laying there did not look natural. People say, "rest in peace," but she did not look at peace. Nothing about her looked real except for her fingertips. She had rings on every single finger. I gripped her casket to keep my balance. Her fingertips were the only thing that verified that yes, this is her and this is really happening. Her nail polish looked picked off, by her I am assuming. Her nails were bitten down to the nub. I had never paid much attention to her nails, but I knew she bit them.

While I was standing there, Scott's sister added yet another ring to her finger. She touched her and was not afraid. I was, but I don't know why. She just slipped it on like it was nothing and walked away. There were small teddy bears in there with her and a photo of her and Scott. Across the top of the casket was a beautiful arrangement of flowers and a banner that said, "Beloved daughter, sister and friend." When I could finally speak, I whispered to Viv, "It doesn't even look like her."

The fact that her forehead looked entirely unreal was just a constant reminder of the head trauma she must have endured. My sweet friend, why did this happen to you?

Once Viv and I had stood there for long enough, we turned around to leave. When I looked up, Kristina was standing there, off to my left and in front of me. I don't know how long she was standing there. I hadn't noticed her at all.

Her face was a hot mess. Clearly she had been crying. Mascara was all running down her face. I don't know how long she and Michaela had been friends, but she was probably the equivalent to what Viv was to me. Her presence took me by surprise. The last time we had any contact with each other was when she shoved one of her friends into me in the hallway in order to knock me over. We both knew that Michaela invited me to go to Cedar Point on Wednesday, but I had backed out. She might have been the last person to see Michaela alive. I wonder what kind of guilt she must have felt. Could she have stopped her? Maybe she could have invited her to stay the night? Did she blame me because she knew my house was on Michaela's way home and I could have driven with her? Had she thought about this as closely as I had? I'm sure she had a million questions too.

It was strange when our eyes met. See, you need to understand girl drama. When girls hate each other, it's for life. It is likely that had this never happened, even though Michaela and I made up, if I would run into Kristina somewhere, like a store or something, even if we had both graduated from high school, we would still glare at each other. It's the silent code of girl drama. In other words, it's a freaking miracle that Michaela and I made up months before.

I have no idea what came over me, but I reached out to hug her. Again, I think the soul somehow instinctively knows what to do and when. I knew to stop crying at Michaela's house when we visited her mom. I take that back. *I* did not know that. My soul did. Now my soul was doing it's thing once again. *I* did not want to hug her, but my soul knew it was what I needed to do, so it happened. It wasn't much of a hug, cordial if anything. I had never been to a calling hours before and did not know what was protocol. I hugged her, whispered that I was so sorry and called it a day.

My heart really did go out to her. I could not imagine losing Viv like this. Michaela and I were friends for such a short time and my heart was shattered. We were super close for the timeframe that she graced my path prior to it all falling apart. But Viv? If this had happened to Viv? I visibly shook my head in an attempt to get the thought out of my head. This can never happen again. I'll spend my life protecting everyone else if I have to.

We turned to leave once again. Dean was standing in line. I gasped and dropped my tissues to the floor. I practically ran to him.

He was much taller than me, so I buried my face into the spot just above his belly button but still under his chest.

"You didn't believe me," I cried.

"I know, I know. I'm sorry," he whispered as tears ran down his face. "The two of you were such idiots when you were together. This is all so stupid. I can't believe this."

"She didn't honk her horn and this is why! Oh my gosh, Dean, we could have called 911 or something. Maybe there was time to save her if we would have called."

"Don't be stupid. You had no idea what happened. If you would have called 911, what would you have said? "My friend didn't honk her horn by 1am, can you go check on her please?""

I knew he was right. Somehow I would have to stop blaming myself for this. It was hard. Life is so strange. One wrong decision can cause a death. Really? Is this how the game of life is played? If I turn left I might die? If I turn right I might live, but as humans we will never know which way we should go until we go. Every little minor decision can equal this. So what do we do? Think through every single decision and all of its possibilities? Like if I have a choice to eat chips or peanuts. Do I need to think through which food is more likely to kill me?

I looked up at Dean and he wiped my tears away with a tissue that he had in his hand. He shook his head as if just as confused as I was. He looked into my teary eyes for a moment. I felt Viv tug on my hand, and I walked out with her. Dean and I would never speak to each other ever again.

Chapter 10: Since You're Gone

"Since you're gone, the nights are gettin' strange
Since you're gone, well, nothing's makin' any sense…"

I was very naive at the age of 16. I had no idea that there were calling hours and then a funeral too. I thought maybe I was *at* the funeral, but I wasn't. There was more.

The following day, Viv drove us to Michaela's church. I wore the same outfit again, since I had no fashion sense. I guess it could have been worse. I could have shown up in jeans and a t-shirt. Worrying about what to wear to a friend's funeral was the least of my worries.

We walked in. The sanctuary was kind of small actually. I had only been to my grandmother's church and one other church at Easter time. Both of those churches were huge, but this one was small. You could maybe squeeze 100 people in there if they sat really close. It wasn't an elaborate church with stained glass windows. The decor was out of date and pretty simple. There was no way all the people from yesterday were going to fit in this room. There was no casket either, which I was kind of okay with. I had seen enough.

We took a seat, half way down and to the right. There was soft music playing. No one spoke. Not even Viv and me. We always had something to talk about, but there was nothing now. And by looking around, I was thinking that you just don't talk at this kind of event. Yesterday was for talking and sharing and hugging and crying. This was a little more formal, for lack of a better word.

All there was to do was to listen to the music that was playing. The song was an old one, The Rose sung by Bette Midler. It was on replay.

> *Some say love, it is a river*
> *That drowns the tender reed*
> *Some say love, it is a razor*
> *That leaves your soul to bleed*
> *Some say love, it is a hunger*
> *An endless aching need*
> *I say love, it is a flower*
> *And you, its only seed*

There was no escaping this song. There was nothing to occupy my mind, only this song engraving itself onto my heart and into my brain. I must have listened to it about 8 times while sitting there. Without any warning, the doors at the back of the church dramatically flew open. It made me jump. It was an odd sound to hear in a place that was supposed to be so peaceful.

Michaela's mom was there standing behind the closed casket which was now on wheels. I don't remember if anyone was helping her to push it because all I remember was seeing her, bent over the top of it as if hugging it for the last time. There was no way she was going to push it herself.

Somehow the casket made it to the altar. The minister said some words and had us all pray. It was all really dizzying. The next thing I knew I was in a line of cars that paraded along the country roads to bury my friend.

The drive seemed to last forever and was unfamiliar even though the cemetery is in my hometown. Everything was a blur and at times, tears filled my eyes so I couldn't see clearly. We got out of the car and stood with the others who were already gathering by the grave.

Again, it was a gorgeous day. Not too hot or cold. There was a slight breeze and not a cloud in the sky. Michaela's casket was at the front of the now smaller crowd. The large flower arrangement was placed on top of it from the funeral home.

The minister said more words and quoted some Bible verses that seemed completely irrelevant. I don't blame him. Someone has to say something. Humans need words to fill the emptiness. When he was finished, he stepped off the podium and left us to fend for ourselves.

There were now no words to fill the space. We all stood there staring at her casket. Everyone was crying. You could hear people quietly crying in agony. Some people were unable to catch their breath. I, too, was crying, but did you know it is possible to run out of tears? My face, I assume, was scrunched up as if crying. My heart was aching like it does when I've cried in the past. The knot in my stomach that I carried with me quite frequently lately was there. I had all the signs of crying, yet no tears were coming from my eyes. I had run completely dry.

Putting your life together after a friend dies is a really strange thing. She didn't live with me, so I can't even imagine what it would be like losing someone you lived with. We weren't back to school yet, so it's not like I would round the corner and see her in her normal spot with her friends in the morning. There was no routine where I knew I was supposed to see her and then be reminded that she was gone. Since we were not back to school, there would be no empty seat to look at. These were all good things. See, if something happened to Viv, I would definitely notice. She takes me to school everyday and brings me home. On any given afternoon, she would be at my house or I would be at hers. The fact that Michaela and I had no routine together was actually kind of helpful. The only routine we had was that she would wail on her horn at 1am each night. Dean and I weren't talking anymore so on the nights that I could sleep, I wouldn't be awake at the hour that she would have driven by.

I was okay with not talking to Dean anymore. It was an unspoken agreement. He was fun to talk to at night after going out with my own friends. He was like the after party. I think we both knew that our conversations were not going to be fun anymore.

Sleeping was never something I was good at. As a child, I was always afraid of everything. You know how most kids love swimming? Not this one. I was terrified of water. I can clearly remember my father, in the water and holding the tips of my fingers, encouraging me to take the leap. I would cry and whine. I was afraid of dogs. I was afraid of eating new foods, which is why I eat the same thing for breakfast every morning since I was a child. This was something I could control and it was safe. I was always afraid of getting kidnapped or something. I was also afraid to sleep. My first nightmare ever was when I was about six years old. I looked over and on my pillow was an ant the size of a watermelon. It was the first nightmare I had ever had that ripped me out of my sleep. After that, I slept with one of my parents until I was about 9 years old. The agony I must have caused them. Now I had a new thing to add to the list. I was afraid of losing yet another friend to a car accident.

The nights after Michaela's funeral were tough. I didn't want to close my eyes because when I did, I saw her face, all fake and made up while she lay in her casket. Why was that the vision that my brain wanted to hold on to? Amy and Viv took turns staying the night at my house until school started back up again which was a good thing. If I woke up in the middle of the night, I would know that they were there and alive.

Eventually, nightmares would terrorize me. Almost every time it was just her in a room that looked like a lab with her laying on a metal examining table. I don't get why my sleeping brain would cook up such an image since that was never anything I had seen in reality. Often there was blood all over the floor that kept rising up until I would shake myself awake. I'm sure it probably means something because it became the same nightmare over and over and over again. Sometimes there were dreams where the two of us were sitting in these unfamiliar easy chairs just chatting away about the everyday, mundane happenings. These were the best. In these dreams I would tell Michaela about what was happening on General Hospital, our favorite soap opera. I would tell her about Matt and Charlene and all of the other new friends I made since she left. These dreams were good for my soul. If only I had more control over them. I would choose those dreams over the bloody nightmares any day.

If God was watching over me, he definitely sent some angels to do the work. Amy and I were very close. The last few weeks of summer and into my junior year were healing for me. Amy and I were together everyday and night, which took me off Viv's hands for a little while. Viv and I still talked and always remained friends. She had seen me through the worst of it. Amy, without her even realizing it, kept my mind occupied.

We would go to work at Cedar Point together until the summer ended. Afterwards we would ride the rides together, eat caramel apples and Cedar Point's world famous fresh cut fries. There was a bar that we would go to after hours with the staff. Don't ask how I managed to get in there. Maybe I looked older than I was, but no one asked to see my driver's license. I still didn't even have a driver's license, just my temps. Those days were thankfully carefree. Of course I still thought of Michaela, especially at night, with Amy by my side. I thought of her every single time I got in the car. Back in those days, you could pretty much get away with not wearing a seatbelt. It wasn't a law. Now, I was wearing one every time I got into a car, and would insist that everyone else in the car put theirs on too, no matter how annoying I was.

Viv and I would hang out too from time to time. There wasn't much to do in our town except maybe drive around, get some fast food and walk around Kmart. One summer afternoon, Viv and I went tooling around with Samson and Rex. He was tall and thin and had short hair. He would wear his hat backwards pretty much all the time. He often wore jeans or camo pants and a different concert t-shirt each day under his stone washed denim jacket. He had a smooth tone to his voice and didn't talk very loud. He often had a look on his face like he was probably thinking about something that he shouldn't be thinking. He was quietly hilarious and wrote funny poetry like "The Virgin Stripper."

Rex, on the other hand, seemed more innocent. He was quiet and kind. When he spoke, it was usually something pretty insightful. Often he was funny and could really get me going. He would do off the wall things like let his dog go at it on his leg simply because it made me laugh hysterically. He could move his hair as if separated from the rest of his head too. He was hilariously, yet quietly entertaining. Rex made me laugh, not with his words so much, but with his stupid human tricks which never ceased to amaze me.

On this lazy summer day, Samson took us to McDonald's to get some food in his sweet red Tempo. He was going to go off to the army at the end of the summer, so he was really living it up! We listened to tunes by Bel Biv DeVoe like "Poison", Bobby Brown's "My Prerogative," and we would play the heck out of Vanilla Ice's classic tape "To the Extreme." My favorite was when he could crank up "Yo Vanilla." The song's original lyrics start off with "Yo Vanilla, kick it 1 time boy!" Samson would always change that line to "Yo, Samson, kick it 3 times maaaaaannnnn." I still hadn't tried a Big Mac yet. I stayed loyal to my 6 piece chicken McNuggets, with hot mustard and sweet and sour sauce, fries, and an ice cold Coca Cola. On a good day I'd order myself a hot fudge sundae with nuts.

After we were all full, we headed over to Kmart. Why? Because like I said, there was nothing else to do. We just walked around and looked at stuff and did not buy anything. If we were lucky, we would catch a blue light special! We weren't interested in buying the special item of the day, but it sure was fun watching the people run through the store frantically to see what was on sale for only a few quick minutes! When we finished perusing the store and checking out what the blue light special was (it was a set of knives if you were wondering). We were out the door.

Sometimes Kmart would put cases of pop outside of the building, in the front, right by the doors. There would be lots of cases. Sometimes it was Coke or Pepsi, other times it was Sunkist or root beer. There would be a huge sign on the cases letting shoppers know it was on sale. Today it was Pepsi. I never understood why Kmart would do this. Wouldn't someone steal the pop? Of course they would, and today that person was Samson. He over confidently walked over to the cases of pop and grabbed one. He had it tucked under his arm, kind of like how one would hold onto a football. He looked around, trying to act casual.

"Yeah, I bought this," he said, to no one.

Kharma has a funny way of working. He looked both ways before he took off to get to the parking lot. He was also checking to see if anyone saw him. For some odd reason, the bottom of the box of Pepsi unexpectedly gave out and the cans started rolling all over the cement. He tried desperately to inconspicuously grab the cans as they were pouring out all over the ground, faster than he could keep up. They were rolling everywhere and he was trying so hard not to look suspicious. It wasn't working and he kept going, looking all around to see if anyone was watching. He was able to manage to hang onto about 6 cans at most. The rest of us weren't going to help him because we didn't want to have any part of it. We weren't going down with him if he got caught. We stood there, by the building and watched it all play out. The funny thing is that if he wanted to look as if he had bought them, it probably would have been best to stop and pick up the cans. I mean, in all reality, IF you paid for them, you would want to get your money's worth. Any innocent paying customer would not walk into Kmart, pay for a case of pop and then leave the cans rolling all over the place. You would pick them up.

Not Samson. He was too focused on getting into his car as quickly as possible before he was seen. It seemed as if no one else was watching besides us, at least for the moment. He almost made it to his car when the unexpected happened. A woman pushing her own shopping cart saw it all. We could see her coming out of nowhere. As she was edging closer to Samson, she also began looking around to see if anyone saw her. She was looking very suspicious. At first I thought she was going to say something to him or maybe even help him pick up the pop since he "bought" it. Instead, she bent down, scooped up as many cans off the ground that she could, and threw them into her cart. And just like that, she was gone.

It was the funniest thing we had seen in a long time. We could barely keep it together. It felt good for things to be so simple once again. We piled into Samson's car and continued to taunt him all the way home.

That was pretty much how my end of my sophomore into my junior year summer went. It was carefree and low stress. If I wasn't at work, I'd be driving around with friends doing absolutely nothing or hanging out by the pool. I was always either with Viv or Amy and her cousins. It was great!

Once school started back up again, my anxiety took a turn for the worse. The good thing was that no one was bullying me anymore. I would see Michaela's friends gathered by the lockers in the same spot as last year. We didn't even make eye contact. It wasn't weird either. They just blended into the scenery and I did the same. I would go through the motions of going to classes.

On the first day of school, I had study hall in the cafeteria, the same place where Michaela and I got into a fist fight so many months before. It seemed like lifetimes had passed. The milk cooler was still in the same place against the wall. The tables were arranged in the same fashion as last year. I glanced over my shoulder and had a quick look. In my head, I could see the fight start to take place again. I shook it off and looked the other way.

The principal greeted us over the PA system and welcomed us back to school. He acknowledged Michaela's death and we all had a moment of silence. *Breathe.* I would tell myself. *Do not fall apart here.* And I wouldn't. Being back to school was fine. It would be after school that would get to me.

Viv would drive me home like she always did. Until dance team practice started up again, Amy would come over after school. She went to a different nearby school. We hung out, watched TV, joked around and snacked. We'd even do homework from time to time. Around 9pm she would have to leave and panic would set in.

"Just call me as soon as you get home," I'd say, everytime she left. "I will be right here," I'd say pointing at the phone, "waiting for you to call. I won't rest until I know you make it home safe."

Back in the 90's there were no cell phones. If there was, I would probably have her talk to me all the way home so she wouldn't fall asleep. There was no Life 360 app either so I couldn't watch her drive all the way home. I would sit right next to the phone, watch the clock and wait. I never wanted any of my friends to leave me, not in a car anyway. She would make it home just fine, everytime. It would take months for this madness to stop. Lucky for me, she understood, was patient and obeyed. She might have rolled her eyes at me while I wasn't looking, but she understood.

One morning the phone rang around 8am. Strangely, when I picked up the phone, it was Viv's mom.

"Hi, Sandy," she said, with her familiar twang, but not as sing songy as she normally was.

"Hi, Mrs. Barnes. What's going on?" I asked, a little concerned.

"Well, sweetie, Viv was in a car accident." That's all it took. I dropped the phone and left the house in my pj's, again, no shoes and took off down the road.

Chapter 11: Drive

"Who's gonna come around when you break?"

It's strange how the body and mind work. Here I was running on the street without shoes. The road was very solid yet it did not bother me. No tears this time. There was no time for that. It was a warm Sunday morning in October. Again, beautiful weather. If you aren't from Northeastern Ohio, let me tell you something about our weather. Come October, typically the grayness of the clouds start kicking in and it stays that way until at least June. Not today. It was sunny and warm with a breeze. Perfect weather for Ohio. Is this how it's going to be every time a friend of mine gets killed in a car accident? Oh the irony!

It didn't take long to get there on foot. I ran through the garage door, clean as a whistle as always. I burst through the kitchen door out of breath. I must have teleported or something because when I got into the kitchen, Mrs. Barnes was just hanging up the phone. Maybe she was having another conversation since I left the house, but it sure looked like I got there in the timeframe of me dropping the phone on my end and her hanging up.

I was so out of breath that I was unable to speak. Her dad was in his rocking chair, enjoying his coffee and looking out the back patio door. The damn cuckoo clock was going off and the grandfather clock was too. Do they not realize I am reliving this nightmare again? Shut up for once, geez! Otherwise, the house was quiet.

"Honey, come here," Mrs. Barnes said, arms open to receive me. I had no choice but to collapse into her arms. I was out of breath and exhausted. Because I was finished running like a mad woman, I was able to finally release tears. I couldn't speak.

"Mom! Mom!" It was Viv! She was clearly in pain from whatever happened. She hobbled into the kitchen.

I looked over at her, confused.

"Mom! What did you tell her?"

"I told her you were in an accident."

"Oh my gosh. I told you not to tell her that! I told you to say that I was alright FIRST and then you could tell her. Oh Lord... Get in here," she commanded.

We both walked into her room. I immediately collapsed on her bed and laid there in a fetal position. I wasn't crying anymore, but I was doing that unrhythmic breathing thing that I do when I flip out.

"What in the world did my mom say to you?" she asked, sitting at the foot of the bed.

"She...she..." I couldn't even get the words out.

"Calm down," she said.

After a few deep breaths, I told her. "She said you got in an accident, so I assumed..." I couldn't speak the words out loud.

"Did my mom not tell you that I was fine?"

"No, she didn't, but I never gave her the chance. As soon as I heard her say you were in an accident, I dropped the phone and ran over."

"Look at me," she said, pressing on her chest, legs and face as if to prove to me she was really right there. "I'm fine."

"I know," I said quietly.

How long was I going to be a complete wreck? How many more accidents and deaths would I have to endure? Would I ever stop being this annoying person that I was becoming? Always anxious? Always scared? Always demanding that my friends call me right when they get home like someone's mother?

Apparently when Terrence drove her home last night, a man was walking in the middle of the road. The man was drunk and decided to play chicken with Terrence's car, a '79 Nova. Terrence swerved to the left to avoid him, but so did the man, so he swerved to the right with the hopes of missing him again. The man mimicked the car's movement and he shifted towards the right. That left Terrence no choice but to go off the road and into a ditch, leaving the man unscathed. The car flipped and the passenger's side, where Viv would normally sit, was smashed in.

"Luckily we weren't fighting because otherwise, I would have been sitting where the car was smashed in."

They had been fighting lately, but when they were getting along, they were in love, like really nacho cheesy love. So when Terrence drove, she just *had* to be by his side so he could put his arm around her. There was no seatbelt where she was sitting. This actually saved her life.

Viv had to miss a week's worth of dance team practice. She wasn't badly injured, but just a little sore. We were settling into our new school routines and things were pretty uneventful. When I didn't have dance team practice, I worked on getting my driver's license.

I wasn't a very good driver. I wasn't a bad driver either. I was a nervous driver. I didn't like the radio to be on and I sat real close, too close, to the dashboard. I think I felt if I could get really close, I could see better.

I never enjoyed getting my driving hours. My driving instructor was kind of a tool. He was young, probably in his early twenties, maybe, but was still kind of immature for a driving instructor. He was shockingly relaxed considering he put his life in danger everyday as his career choice. He was probably stoned most of the time. Driving instructors should definitely take their job a little more seriously than this guy. In fact, I am betting that they don't get paid much and they should!

He was overweight and kind of dirty. He wasn't huge, just soft. He usually wore an unclean shirt that was slightly too small. Every now and again, if he moved just right, I'd catch a glimpse of his hairy belly button as it drooped over his jeans. He had a denim jacket with Motley Crue pins all over the front. I am guessing he was probably out drinking the night before and simply fell asleep in his clothes. He always smelled a little like stale beer, dirty clothes and body odor. It was gross and I'd have to spend 2 hours every Saturday with this guy until I reached all of my hours.

Every session was pretty much the same. I'd get into the driver's seat and pull on my seatbelt. He did not. He'd move the seat back so that he could fit into the passenger's seat. I moved the driver's seat forward so I could reach the pedals. Sometimes he would crack the window and smoke a cigarette. He would stare out the window casually and share a driving tip here and there. Otherwise, we didn't really talk which I was glad for. I wasn't good with casual conversation, and I was too nervous when I drove to talk. I didn't want anything to distract me from the road. Sometimes he'd even let me fend for myself. He'd lean his seat back, take off his ball cap and place it over his face to take a little snooze. He definitely did not take pride in his job. He was getting a paycheck, probably for beer, and for him it was easy. Clearly he didn't care about his own well being. If I had to get into a car with a new driver for my job daily, I would be terrified. Honestly, it was the perfect situation for him. Saturdays were probably the only day he'd have to get up early, which was 10AM. Otherwise, I picture him drinking all day while we were at school until he'd have another "client" in the afternoon and evening.

One night I was out with Amy while she was driving. We were stopped at a stoplight. I looked over and saw my driving instructor in a car with one of his friends. He was in the passenger seat moving his hand around in a circle to signal me to roll down my window.

"Uh, hey," I said, uncomfortably.

"Hey!" he said obnoxiously. "I've been drinking. Shhhhhhh!" as he put his index finger up to his lips, laughing.

"I see that."

"Don't tell," he whispered, and his friend drove away laughing.

There he goes, I thought to myself. *My driving instructor. His mother must be so proud.* After failing the written and the driving portion of the test once, I finally passed. The state of Ohio allowed me, of all people, to drive on the roads.

For my junior year, we got new dance team uniforms. My freshman year we wore these skin tight, God awful dance costumes. The bodysuits were white with long, puffy sleeves. Then we put on this hideous vest over it that had red and black sequins. Depending on the dance routine, we'd either wear black dance pants or this silky, flowy black skirt. My sophomore year was better. We had a one piece, red bodysuit with skin tight long sleeves, not puffy this time. The attached short skirt would flare out and don't forget the sequins. Instead of having sequins all over it, it just said "Falcons" in shiny silver.

This year we decided it would be best to look more like cheerleaders for some reason. We ordered white tops with no sleeves that had a red F on the front in a varsity font. The pleated skirt, also white, had black and red trim on the bottom. Not too shabby. At least I didn't feel like I looked like a figure skater.

I got a phone call later in the evening from my friend Tabitha. She was calling to let me know that the new uniforms were in and our coach wanted me to get over there quickly to pick it up. She wanted us to be able to wear them to school the following day, since our first performance would be that night. It was already kind of late for a school night. My mom wasn't happy that I was going to drive at night as a new driver, but I begged her to let me. All the other girls had their uniforms already and were set to wear them in the morning. I didn't want to be left out.

Ignoring my mother's disapproving looks, I headed out the door. I never liked disappointing my mother, but tonight I was going to have to suck up the sick feeling I had. I did not want to be the only one on the squad who did not have their new uniform.

I got in the car and pulled on my seatbelt. It was already dark since it was around 8pm on this cool November evening. I didn't even throw on a jacket, I was in such a hurry. I figured I'd just put the heat on in the car and run into my coach's house.

As soon as I pulled out of my driveway and onto the road, I had the realization that this was the first time I had ever driven alone at night. Things look very different from the driver's seat when it's dark. My seat was pulled up pretty close to the dashboard as always. I checked to see if I could move any closer just to be sure I was able to see as clearly as possible. Unfortunately I couldn't move any closer or else my knees would be pressed up to the dash. At least if I stayed the way I was, my knees only brushed against it. Now I know, I can't see any better if I moved even a millimeter closer. It just felt safer and secure if I was as close as I could be.

The car was silent and since our town is pretty small, there were barely any cars on the road. My coach lived just outside of town. I didn't turn the radio on. I wanted nothing to distract me. Actually I was kind of getting scared. I have a very vivid imagination, and don't forget, when I was little, I was afraid of everything. Even if there was nothing going on that was scary, my mind had the capability to dream up the most awful things, just to make sure I was paying attention.

It felt like someone was in my backseat. I tried looking in my rear view mirror, but I couldn't see anything. Any little sound my blue Ford Taurus made caused me to jump. I decided to reach back with my right arm to see if I could feel the intruder. Maybe he was crouched down in a ball right behind me, waiting until I got to a stop sign and then he would hijack my car. I swung my arm back and forth in the back seat. This was a super strange position for my body to be in. I was a devout hands at 10 o'clock and 2 o'clock driver. I had never driven with one hand. I was always too nervous to let go of the steering wheel. Typically I would have my hands clenched around the steering wheel, tight enough that my knuckles would turn white.

My hand brushed up against something and I let out an audible gasp. It's a murderer! No, it's a demon who came up from the underworld to kill me! I know it is! I can feel its evil presence! I decided that I had to take a look. While driving, I took a quick look over my shoulder. You wouldn't believe what it was. It was my backpack. When I turned back around, I was headed towards someone's mailbox, so I quickly swerved to the left, but a little too much. I went half way into the other lane. Thankfully, no one was coming. By now, both hands were tightly clenched around the wheel once again. I was sweating with fear and breathing heavily, but was now a little relieved that it wasn't a murderer or worse, a demon from the pits of Hell.

I was taking some deep breaths and after a few minutes in the silence, I started to breathe normally again. I still felt the presence of something. I decided it would be best to just focus on the road and think of nothing but the road.

Instead, I started thinking about how much my mother would kill me if I would have hit that mailbox. My parents just got this car for me. I hated getting in trouble with my parents. My mother would loudly yell at me. She had a way with just her tone of voice and choice of words that made fear run through my very soul. However, it never stopped me from getting in trouble, I reflected. There was a constant struggle within me between getting in trouble with my mother versus going out and having fun with my friends. I would just do my thing and hope for the best. Sometimes I'd get caught, like when we decided to get into the car with the 18 year old boy who was dumb enough to give a bunch of 8th grade girls beer. Sometimes I wouldn't get caught, and I'd end up at one of Michaela's really fun parties.

Michaela. My mind would wander to her every day, especially when I put on my seatbelt. I swore I would always wear my seatbelt after Michaela's accident and vowed to make everyone in the car with me do the same. Time had wiped the tears away, but it would never be able to wipe away the memories: the good, the bad or the ugly.

I was about 5 minutes from my coach's house. I was coming towards a stop light at the top of a hill. It wasn't a super tall hill or anything. The road simply dipped down just a little, then went up slightly to the stoplight. The road would dip down again on the other side once I'd make it past the light. The thing is, I never did. I never made it past the light.

I was going pretty slow, maybe 25mph at best. The light was green so I was going to have to make a rolling left turn. I looked out in front of me and saw nothing, so I made the left turn. Out of nowhere, literally, out of nowhere, a car plowed into me practically head on. The other car was going so fast that when it hit me, my car spun completely around and I was facing the way I had just driven.

Imagine all I am about to say going in slow motion, because for me, that's how I was seeing it play out. When I started to make the rolling left turn, the overly bright headlights were shining right in my eyes. I could see them get brighter and brighter, and in the meantime, my entire life flashed before my eyes. This is a real thing. I've heard the expression, "my life flashed before my eyes" at some point in my life, but I thought it was just a figure of speech. It's not. It really can happen because it did for me.

In just this one millisecond, as the lights were coming towards me, I saw my parents and my brother. I saw Viv and Amy and even Michaela. I saw my birth. I saw my mother holding me in her hospital bed, moments after she brought me into the world. I saw graduation, my wedding and my unborn children. Next I saw my head go for the window. *This is it.* I thought. *This is how it's going to end.* I squinted and braced myself for impact. Life continued to flash before my eyes. I saw Viv and Amy hugging at my funeral. I saw my mother's disgruntled face flash by because she never wanted me to go in the first place. *Great.* I thought again. *If I live through this, I will have to deal with her. Maybe this won't be so bad if I don't make it.* I saw all of this all the while the lights were getting closer and closer. *Maybe I'm dead?* I kept thinking. *If I am, this actually isn't too bad. Nothing hurts. I see the bright lights. Am I dead?*

Suddenly, life stopped flashing before my eyes. *Okay, so now I'm dead,* I thought to myself. I felt lots of pressure against my chest. I couldn't move. I didn't see the bright lights anymore. *Oh no! I'm in Hell! I laughed at too many Helen Keller jokes! I knew it!*

Well, I wasn't in Hell. I wasn't in Heaven either. I opened my eyes. In front of me was the familiar little country store. It was closed. The lights were out and there were no cars in the parking lot. It took me a moment to get my bearings.

After a few moments of taking it all in, I soon realized that my car was facing the way I had come. I didn't see any cars on the road, just the country store and a few homes on either side of the street. It was dark with the only street light shining in the country store's parking lot. It was so eerily quiet that I could hear the stop light click when it would change from green to yellow to red. What just happened?

I looked down and blood was soaking into my cotton pants that I was wearing. I had just gotten this outfit too. My mom had gotten a magazine in the mail and I was perusing through it while eating breakfast one morning. It was a white sweater that went past the waist. It had army green swirls inside of a rectangle on the front. The cotton pants were also army green and had the same swirly pattern on them. I asked her to get it for me and she did! I loved this outfit. Today was the first day I had ever worn it. Now the pants that I loved were soaking up with blood, right before my eyes, yet I didn't feel any pain. The dashboard was crooked. The passenger's side was smashed inward by a few inches.

I looked around. I knew I was hit by another car, but where was it? I looked to the left and to the right and there were no cars. Next, I tried to pull myself up a bit so that I could look behind me. My knees were pinned against the dashboard. My seatbelt was locked hard against my chest.

I unbuckled it. That helped a little. I was at least able to pull my upper body up just enough to look behind me.

It was there. There was a crack in the window along with a circular spider web type crack where the driver's head must have hit the windshield. There was blood sprayed all over the window and some of it was dripping down. I couldn't see the driver very clearly, but I could see her long hair and the top of her head draped over the steering wheel. She wasn't moving. She wasn't making any sounds at all from what I could hear. I only heard crickets.

It was then that I realized that I killed her.

Chapter 12: Double Life

*"You think it's a phase, and it's all gonna happen to you
When you drive in the haze..."*

I didn't know what else to do. I couldn't move. I was starting to flip out but somehow I managed to figure out that now was not a good time to do that. I was alone. It was late. There were no cell phones in the early 90's so I couldn't call for help. I saw a payphone in the parking lot of the little country store. *If I can get to it, I will dial 911,* I thought to myself. The problem was, I couldn't move. I was starting to feel some pain, but the reason I couldn't move was because the dash had pinned my legs up against the seat. I managed to roll my window down and started screaming for help.

"HELP! HELP!" I screamed. "PLEASE SOMEONE HELP!" It felt like forever, and no one was coming. I looked behind me again, and the girl was still there, not moving. I thought maybe there was a small chance that my screams would awaken her, but that was not the case. I kept yelling and yelling until finally I ran out of breath. I was getting scared. My pants were getting bloodier by the second. I survived this, and now my mom was going to kill me. I started to cry. No one was coming. I just sat there, eyes closed and tears running down my face and onto my new white sweater.

Eventually, someone finally drove by and pulled over. "HELP! HELP PLEASE!" I started screaming.

"Are you okay?" the stranger asked. It was a man. He looked a little younger than my parents. He had dark eyes and pale skin. He had on a green winter jacket and a light brown hat. I could see his breath as he spoke. There was a woman behind him, peeking her head in trying to see me. She had a look of concern.

"I think I am okay, but please, go check on the other girl. I am fine."

"Okay", they nodded, and took off.

I couldn't see what was going on. I was just grateful that someone else was there. My window was still down, so I could hear a little bit of what was going on, but just barely.

"Oh my God," I heard the woman say. "Go call 911. There's a phone over there."

Even though I was facing the other way, my mind kept showing me the other girl, all bloody and not moving. What had I done? I started thinking about her family and how my mom was going to be so upset with me. Here I had killed someone, and all I could think about was what my mother was going to do to me. How pathetic is that?

Far off in the distance I finally heard sirens. Since I couldn't move, I couldn't get a good look around. I could see the red and blue shadows of the lights reflecting off of my car and into my window and danced across my dashboard. A paramedic came to my window.

"Are you okay?" he said. I started getting all worked up again.

"I am, but I am worried about the other girl. Please, please go over there and take care of her. She isn't moving"

"Someone is over there with her. I need to get you out of this car." He opened the door.

"I'm going to move your seat back, so just be still," he said, as if there was another option. Slowly my seat was edging back.

"I'm going to have to cut these pants open so I can see your injuries."

"Oh heck no! You can't do that! My mother is going to go through the roof. She just bought these. This is the first time I ever wore them. You can't do that!" I yelled. I had to have sounded so ridiculous to him, but I was terrified of my mother. He didn't understand.

"Look sweetie, your mom's not going to care. She is just going to be happy you are alive," he said.

"Once she realizes that I am alive, she's going to kill me. Please don't cut them off. At least help me slide them off," I begged. "Maybe I can wash the blood out."

By now, the pants were ruined. There was no way to save them. Even if I tried to wash them, they would still be stained with blood. Luckily I couldn't move and the paramedic was already cutting the pants from my thigh down.

I saw the gurney and a long wooden board. He put my head into some kind of brace. All I could do was watch all of this unfold like an outsider. Another paramedic showed up. They carefully placed my body on the board and then slid me onto the gurney and strapped me in. I didn't see the other girl, just her car.

Once in the back of the ambulance, I had settled down a little. They gave me oxygen and the paramedic said I was going to be fine. Interestingly enough, I didn't feel much. Adrenaline must be magical or something. He tended to my wounds and wiped the blood off.

The ride wasn't that long. They took some x-rays and nothing seemed to be broken. After what felt like an eternity, they finally let my parents in.

Shockingly, they didn't say much. I was pretty sure they were disappointed. I should have listened to my mother, or maybe she should have just taken me, but at the time, I was insisting on driving myself. She was already in her pajamas and I didn't feel like suggesting it when I knew I could drive myself.

"I'm sorry I ruined my new pants," I said to my mom. I was still laying in the emergency room bed. My parents were standing over me. My mother's arms were folded and she was looking down at me. Even now, she still looked disapproving. Maybe she just always looked that way, I resolved. I mean, either I was always disappointing her, or literally, that's just how she looked.

The doctor said I badly bruised my knees and suggested that in the future I should move my seat back a little more. I had no broken bones, but he said I would more than likely be sore in the morning. I had been so distracted with my own well being that I had forgotten that I had killed someone.

It was late by the time we got home. Thankfully my parents didn't say much. I thought for sure they were going to be mad at me, but they weren't. We were all really tired, so we quickly went to bed.

My body still didn't hurt as much as you would think it should. My beautiful new pants were covered in blood, but it definitely was not a reflection of my injuries. Both knees were badly scraped, probably the worst scrape I had ever had in my life, but nothing major, at least not tonight. The police said had I not had my seatbelt on, I would not have made it and probably would have died upon impact.

It was quiet in the house and dark. My body felt exhausted, but my mind could not rest. Because everything was so fast paced at the emergency room, I never had a chance to really reflect on what I had done.

I made that left turn, but I remember distinctly double checking to make sure no one was there. I was such a paranoid driver. I would check all around me if I was driving in a school zone at precisely 25mph. Michaela's accident had scared me to death. I was always very careful. Right before I was going to turn left, I didn't even see a shimmer of light. Where in the world did this car come from?

Thinking about the blood splattered on the windshield and the girl and her hair flopped over the top of her head was maddening. Who was she? How old was she? I assumed she was young. Maybe she wasn't? Maybe she was a mother? Oh my gosh did I take someone's mother? My mother drove me crazy, but I couldn't imagine living without her. What if she was a teenager like Michaela? I had seen what death does to a mother. Did I cause that to happen to her mother?

Laying there in the quiet and still darkness, I couldn't rest. Every time I closed my eyes I saw the girl or the woman that I killed that night. Since life was full of tragedies lately, I had learned to take deep breaths when I started to get worked up again. Everytime a new tragic event happened, people were telling me to take deep breaths, so I tried it. It was working a little, but not enough. I decided to call Viv.

"Hey," I said wearily when she picked up the phone on the first ring.

"Well, it's about time you called!" she said.

"I take it you already know what happened."

"Yeah. Your mom called my mom. She said you were okay. Are you?" she asked.

"My body is okay, if that's what you mean. My new outfit was ruined. They had to cut it off of me. Can you believe that? My mom wasn't even mad either, thank God!"

"So what are your injuries?" she asked.

"My knees are all scraped up. They have them both wrapped up in gauze and they gave me these huge bandaids."

"You sit too close to the dashboard. I told you that. You don't need to sit that close. You are lucky you aren't paralyzed," she scolded.

"Viv, that isn't even the worst of it. Did my parents tell your mom that I killed someone tonight?" I shuddered at the thought.

"Uh, no," she said, waiting for me to go on.

"The girl I hit died. I'm a murderer," I said, wanting to vomit.

"You're not a murderer. It was an accident."

"Viv, am I going to go to prison?" It dawned on me that I might. Beth's husband did. When he hit the guy on the bike, that was an accident, but he was drinking, so maybe that was different.

"You're not going to go to prison," she said.

"Will went to prison for killing that other guy with his car. How is this any different?" I asked nervously.

"Were you drunk?"

"Well, no," I said.

"Well then you aren't going to go to prison. You're not even old enough to go to prison."

"Well, what about juvie then? Won't I go to juvie?" We heard about how bad kids went to the juvenile detention hall. What I did was pretty bad.

"I don't know," Viv said. "I doubt it. The kids that go to juvie mean to do bad things. You didn't mean to do this."

She had a good point. Viv was always the voice of reason. I don't know how she could put up with me. I guess it was probably because we were more like sisters. You can't stop being sisters.

"You should really try to go to sleep," she said.

"I know, but every time I close my eyes I keep seeing the girl, so I don't want to close my eyes." I still suffered from the awful bloody nightmare of Michaela from time to time. I can only imagine what my mind will cook up after what happened tonight. It is so strange what my mind can create, even though I have never seen the things that it creates in my dreams in real life.

"Viv, I'm scared to fall asleep. Can you just come over here?" It was 1am. It was a pretty lofty request.

"No. My parents will not be happy if I wake them up to ask them if I can." I could relate to that. My parents would have told me no too. "Plus, I have to get up for school tomorrow and you don't."

"You're right. Okay, so can you just stay on the phone with me then? Please?" I begged.

"Yeah, just stop talking, okay?" she said.

"Okay, I will, but if I have a nightmare, can I wake you up?"

"Yes," she said, "But try not to have a nightmare," she said, snickering.

"Okay, okay. I'll do my best," I promised. Believe me, I did not want to have a nightmare. I wish I knew what triggered them because if I knew, I would avoid them at all costs.

Soon I heard Viv's familiar deep sleep breathing. It was slow and rhythmic with a hint of a snore. I continued to listen. It was comforting. I must have been pretty tired because I fell asleep too, at least for a little while.

I didn't have any nightmares that night, but I could not rest peacefully. I woke up and reality set in. I glanced at the clock. It was 4am.

Gasping, I woke up Viv. "Viv! Viv!" I whispered loudly. "Viv! Are you still there?" I said. I heard her grumble.

"Yeah. Yeah," she said sleepily. "What is it?"

"Nothing. I just wanted to make sure you were still there. Go back to sleep."

I could almost hear her eyes roll through the phone. I dozed off once again. When I woke, the sun was out and I could hear Viv getting ready for school. I could hear the stupid grandfather clock on the other end, playing its all too familiar and annoying tune. I could hear her walking around in her room. She must have been doing her hair because I could hear the sound of her spraying her hair with hairspray. I felt like a spy listening in. I chuckled a bit to myself. Eventually, Viv picked up the phone.

"Are you awake?" she asked.

"I am."

"What are you doing?"

"I'm listening to you get ready for school," I said.

"You're such a weirdo. I gotta get moving now, okay? I'll stop by after school."

"Okay. Have a good day."

"Okay," she said. "Bye."

The sun was streaming into my room. I could smell my dad making his coffee. He must not have gone into work either. My brother and my mom were gone. Maybe she took him to school.

So much for thinking that I wasn't injured that badly. When I woke up and tried to get out of bed, I was in a ton of pain. My knees were the only thing that really felt any impact from the crash. They were the only things that bled and were covered in bandages, yet my entire body was sore. The doctor had warned me that this would probably happen. My adrenalin must have been done protecting me from the pain. I powered through. I wanted to talk to my dad.

Very slowly I moved towards the door. I was worse than an old person. I know I could have just called for my dad, but I didn't want to be in bed any longer. I discovered that the more I laid there, the more I thought about the girl and the more I would see her head and the blood. If I got up and got moving, maybe my attention would go elsewhere instead of to her. My dad was sitting calmly at the kitchen table with his coffee. I took a seat across from him.

"Dad," I said, nervously. "Am I going to juvie?"

"You mean the juvenile detention center up the road? Why would you think that?"

"Because I killed that girl last night," I said. I hated the sound of it.

"What girl? You killed a girl?" he asked, confused.

"Well, yeah. I hit her with my car. Dad, when I looked at her, there was blood all over the place and she wasn't moving."

"True. But you didn't kill her. She was just knocked out."

You know when people say it was like a weight lifting off their shoulders when they hear good news? I truly felt that way, and I swear because the weight was now gone and was so heavy, I sat a little taller.

"She's going to have to spend a few days in the hospital, but she's going to be okay," he explained.

Wow. I was amazed. I let out an audible sigh of relief. The sight of it was so terrible that I couldn't imagine that anyone could live through the aftermath that I saw.

"Dad, I hurt all over," I told him.

"You should use those crutches," he pointed at the crutches that were leaning against the cabinet where the microwave was. "They gave those to you to use if you needed them. You didn't seem like you needed them last night, so we threw them in the trunk. Try those."

I grabbed them and used them to brace myself. They felt awkward and they did not take the pain off of my entire body, but I had to admit, I could walk with less pain. The pain was much worse when I put pressure on my knees. Using the crutches took the edge off. I made my way into the living room so I could watch TV. My mom had already set up a pillow and a blanket in there for me assuming that this is what I would do. I flipped on the TV and turned on "The Price is Right."

I loved being at home while everyone else had to be at school. I must have dosed in and out of sleep. I was able to catch up on my soap operas. I loved One Life to Live and General Hospital. I felt so relieved that I was not a murderer after all. Eventually I heard a tap on the front door and then

Viv walked in. She sat on the other couch in my living room. She asked me how I was feeling and I gave her an update.

"Everyone thought you died last night," she said.

"Seriously?" I asked, curious and stunned all at once.

"Yeah. I don't know how that rumor got started, but people kept coming up to me telling me that they were sorry for my loss. I was like,"What the heck are you talking about?""

Hmmm….that's interesting.

"Well? What did you tell them?" I asked.

"I told them you were banged up but you were fine. The girl you hit was Tucker Thompson's cousin. Did you know that?"

Tucker Thompson sat in front of me in Government class. He wore the same Tom Petty concert t-shirt everyday to school. I might not have noticed that, but the back of his shirt had some of the lyrics to "The Waiting" and often, when I was not paying attention, which was most of the time, I would read the lyrics: *The waiting is the hardest part. Every day you see one more card. You take it on faith, you take it to the heart…"* He was just sort of your average Joe kind of a guy. He didn't talk much, but sometimes he did something funny that would get us all going.

"I did not know that. I didn't find out anything about her. No one told me. So is she older? Younger? It was hard to tell. There was blood all over her windshield and her head was bent over the steering wheel."

"I think she's a little older than us, like in her 20's maybe."

I wonder if Tucker Thompson hated me now. We weren't really friends in the first place, so probably not. I'm just glad she's going to be okay. I still felt pretty bad about it, but at least she wasn't dead.

Viv and I sat on the couch and chatted. We finished watching General Hospital. Things felt a little more normal, and for that I was thankful.

Chapter 13: You Are the Girl

"You are the girl in my dreams..."

Our junior year ended up being the best year of my life. It was full of parties and prom and fun. I was still paranoid about my friends driving in a car, but they loved me enough to put up with me. I ended up dating Matt for a little while, but then I became the butt of his jokes rather than Helen Keller. In the meantime, Amy, Charlene, Nate and I ended up getting really close.

Amy was a year older than me. She took her first year off after graduation to work and to wait for me to finish up my senior year. Instead of going to college with Michaela, I ended up going with Amy. It was great. Amy always seemed a little more grown up than me, so it was nice to go off to a new place with her rather than alone. We would navigate college life together.

Dorm life for us was awful. The girls that lived next to us hated everything about us. They were bigger than us and had no problem acting like they were going to kill us on any given day. The one girl was about 7 feet tall and thin. Okay, so she probably really wasn't really 7 feet tall, but the way she towered over us made her look like she was. She had really bad dirty blonde mall hair. First of all, she had a bob haircut. Her hair only went down to her chin. Then the mall bangs went straight up to the sky. She took a few of her other bangs and curled them under, so they made a straight line across her forehead. She had beady eyes and a square jaw. Her side kick was no better. She too, had little beady eyes and a mouth that made a permanent frown. She had a bob haircut, chin length, with a really bad home perm. Her mall hair was not as intimidating. It looked like she tried to attempt it, but her mall hair was more like the feathered look from the 80's. She couldn't quite get her bangs to go up to the sky like her leader. Instead, they parted to the left and right which made her bob look more like a triangle. We would call her the "Drowned Rat," behind her back because that was what she looked like. She was much shorter, probably as tall as Amy. The two of them looked like misery.

    I never knew exactly what we did to them to set them off. They would glare at us and mumble "bitch" under their breath when we would walk by. If we were each in our own rooms we could hear them say awful things about us purposefully loud enough so we could hear. Our walls were paper thin, so they could hear us and we could hear them all the time. That was no one's fault. Amy and I never had parties in our tiny dorm room. The drawers on our dressers were somewhat problematic. They were built into the thin wall between our two rooms. If one of us would push the drawer in a little too hard, then the drawer on the other side would pop out. If we really slammed it, we could have probably made their drawer slide across the room. Or, if either of us wanted to, we could pull out the drawers on our side, kick out the drawers on their side and crawl through. It was a really bad design.

Amy and I never wanted any trouble. Before we could turn on our TV or stereo, we would listen through the wall to make sure they were not there so as to not wake the beasts. The bathroom was right across from us, so we would press our ears against the door to make sure there was no one in there before we entered. We never had any major confrontations with them, only the day to day dirty looks and mumbling.

The recurring nightmares about Michaela continued to follow me into college. Finally, one night I had a dream where Michaela and I were hanging out in my dorm room. We were cozy in our sweatpants and college sweatshirts. She had on a red college sweatshirt with the name of the college that we were supposed to go to. I told her everything that was going on in my life. I told her everything from what my classes were like and the food at college. I told her about all the cute guys I was meeting and the girls who continually picked on us. I let it all out. She sat there and patiently listened, smiling, laughing and nodding her head with approval. When I was finished, she was magically transported through the tall window in my dorm room like a ghost. She stood on the ledge. She looked back at me over her left shoulder with that smile that always lit up my world and gave me a wink. Huge, sparkling angel wings emerged from her back. It was kind of funny because she still had on the red sweatshirt and gray sweatpants, but had angel wings all of sudden. She took a graceful leap and went off into the distance. I haven't had a dream about her since.

Chapter 14: Shake It Up

"Dance all night with anyone, don't let nobody pick your fun..."

Amy and I spent a year together at Kent State University. I went there because I had this dream that I was going to follow in Oprah Winfrey's steps and have my own talk show. I don't know why I thought I might be good at this. I stunk at conversation, especially with people I didn't know well. Kent was known for its famous alumni such as Arsenio Hall and Drew Carey. For sure I would be equally as successful if I went there too. I had dreams of having loads of money like Oprah. I would have a special episode where I would have enough money to buy a car for each of my audience members and would hand them out like candy. "Here's one for you, and you, and you," I'd think to myself.

There was an opening for a news anchor for the university's campus news channel. I thought I'd give it a whirl, even though I had no experience in TV at all whatsoever. It was a rude awakening for me.

I was all calm, cool and collected as I waited for my name to be called. I wore my most professional outfit. It was a slim fitting, simple black dress. All I had to do was sit at the desk and read what was on the paper. Sounds pretty easy, doesn't it? Instead, I sat at the desk obediently, started reading from the paper, and looked up. There were lights on me and a big camera pointed at me. They must have wanted to see how I looked on camera. I froze. Instead of reading from the paper, I apologized, told them this was not for me, and I got up and left.

"Maybe you should be a teacher," my mom told me after I finished telling her about my embarrassing exit. I don't know why she thought this would be a good idea. I should ask her one day. I had very little experience with children. I wasn't even smart and I hated school. I thought my mom was crazy, but I knew being in front of a camera was not for me, so I went with it. I had no other plan anyway.

Believe it or not, after college, I became a teacher, a science teacher of all things! I chuckle when I think back to Mrs. Frank's biology class. Once I became a teacher, I made it my philosophy that school was going to be fun, not dreadful like when I was in school. Most days, it is fun. What I realized is that it is up to me to make it that way. I have found my niche for sure, but it took a long time. Sometimes Mother does know best.

Viv, on the other hand, broke up with Terrence for a few months during our junior year. They had been together since they were freshmen. She started hanging out more with Amy, Charlene and me. She started going to parties with us, but was still a little nervous about drinking, which was probably smart. Unfortunately she ended up having a taste of the drama that she had been protected from for years.

Viv was gorgeous and had a rockin' body for a seventeen year old girl. I don't think even she realized how attractive she was since she was always in the clutches of Terrence. She encountered several of Matt and Nate's hot looking friends who were assholes. At first, Viv did not know what to do with all the attention she was getting, however she would quickly find out how much she appreciated how respectful Terrence was to her. He had been her safe place for nearly all of high school. The stress and the drama ended up being too much, so she got back with Terrence. Later, he proposed to her and of course, she said yes.

They went off to college together with the hopes of one day getting married. They were going to be the classic tale of two high school sweethearts, having kids together, living in a little house with a white picket fence. That's not what happened at all. They discovered that there was just too much world that needed to be explored and it had to be done without each other. Even though they broke off the engagement, they remained friends.

Viv went through many bad relationships. She dated all kinds of guys. Carhart wearing guys from home, players from college. Then she quit college and came home. She even dated a rock star and followed him on the road for a few months.

After living the rock star girlfriend life, she finally came home for good. I wasn't around because I was still in college. Terrence stayed at school as well. Things got a little lonely for Viv. She hung out at local bars and eventually met Earle.

I hated Earle. The two of them started drinking. Viv never drank in high school and here she was drinking every night with Earle.

One night she called me at college. When I answered the phone, she was whispering and out of breath.

"Cyn! Cyn!" she whispered, kind of loudly for a whisper.

"What? Huh? Who is this?" I asked, sleepily.

"It's me," she said.

"Who's "me?"" I asked, still not recognizing her whisper.

"It's Viv!" she whispered.

"Why are you whispering?" I asked.

"Because I'm in a cornfield."

"What? What are you doing?" I said, rubbing my eyes.

"Earle and I got into a fight and he was drinking. He threw all of my furniture out the window. He got in the car and I tried to stop him, but the best I could do was just jump in the car with him," she explained.

"You're stupid," I whispered. I didn't want to wake Amy.

"Look, I know. I don't need to hear that right now. I need you to tell me what to do."

"Well first, tell me how you ended up in a cornfield?"

"He was driving really fast, so the cops were chasing us. He pulled over and took off into this cornfield on foot."

"So like, where are you exactly? Are you in the car in the cornfield, or are you like walking around in the corn field?"

"Well, I was walking around in the cornfield because I was running after Earle, but I couldn't find him. The cops are still searching for him. I'm in the car so I could call you," she said. Back then, cell phones were starting to become a thing, but you had to plug it into the lighter in a car. We really called them car phones for the longest time.

"So, tell me what I should do," she was still whispering, which I'm not totally sure why, but the two of us kept whispering.

"I don't know. Let Earle go and go home. That's what you should do," I said.

"Well, what about Earle?" she asked.

"What about him? Take a good look at yourself right now. You are in a cornfield chasing after a drunk who just threw your furniture out the window. He's obviously wanted by the cops or else he wouldn't run. Go home. Go home to your mom's. Don't go back to that shitty apartment that you share with him. Go home."

I could hear her let out a sigh on the other end of the phone.

"You hear me, Viv? Just go home. What else are you going to do?"

"You're right," she said, annoyed with the fact. "It's pretty cold out here, and it looks like I have no other option."

It was all very strange to be on this side of the coin. Viv never really needed me. I was always the one who caused drama or was in the middle of some kind of drama. Viv was a smart girl, except for when it came to guys.

Viv went in and out of many abusive relationships. She would often question if she should give Terrence a call, but she never followed through. Soon enough we found out that he moved out of state and got married.

After her awful night in the cornfield, Viv left Earle. I was shocked. She not only left him, but moved completely out of state to Arizona where she knew no one. She told me she had enough and wanted to start all over. While there, she finished school and got her degree. She met Mack, the man of her dreams, and in this case, they lived happily ever after.

After I graduated from college, I lived at home with my parents for a few weeks while Charlene and I looked for a place to live. Char and I would hang out at the local bar,

Church Street, on Thursday nights. It was a 5 minute drive from my parents' house uptown in Amherst. The townhouse that we found ended up being only about a five minute drive from Church Street as well, which worked out great for us. Just when I thought my bullying days were over, they weren't. I managed to have 1 year off of Tim's daily tormenting in high school since he was a year older and graduated before me. I went away to college for four years without ever running into him when I would come home and visit. Today was different. My little "break" from Tim came to a screeching halt.

When we walked in, he saw me right away. He yelled out my name from the bar where he was sitting, "Well, well, if it isn't good old Ching Chong. I see you never went back to your homeland," he'd yell, in front of everyone. He looked around to see if anyone still thought he was funny. Some chuckled a little, but most smiled uncomfortably. I just ignored him and kept going.

People tell children when they are bullied, if you just ignore them, they will stop. I am sure that worked for some but not for me. There were plenty of times I ignored him on the bus, at school and even at this bar, but in Tim's eyes, my ignoring him was just an invitation to keep going.

I had just sat down and started chatting with a guy I met. Tim came up to the two of us and rudely interrupted me mid sentence.

"You know, I'm sorry I picked on you all those years," he said with a smirk.

He didn't mean it. For someone who disliked me so much, he always seemed to find a reason to speak to me. That's what I don't understand about bullies. I assume they are saying mean and horrible things because they don't like you. I mean, why would you say such awful things to someone you liked? If he didn't like me, why did he spend so much of his time on me? Why did he always seek me out? If my slanted eyes bothered him so much, why did he want to keep looking at them? Even for the amount of time that I didn't like Michaela, I just stopped talking to her (which we all now know, was not a good idea). At least I didn't bully her.

Instead of replying, I acted as if he wasn't there and continued my conversation. When he interrupted me, I stopped my conversation, looked at him while he spoke and then turned back and continued my conversation with a smile. In other words, I acknowledged him with my eye contact, but continued on as if I didn't care what he was saying, which honestly, was kind of the truth. I was so beyond this type of immature behavior. I wasn't going to lose any more of my time to it. He had taken enough of my time all those years, and I wasn't going to get any of it back.

"Hey Ching Chang. Don't you hear me? I'm talking to you," he said. The guy I was sitting with was starting to get annoyed.

Keep in mind, we were over 21 years old at this point. Really? Are we going to keep playing these games?

"I heard you," I said. "I just don't care about what you say, and I really don't care about you."

Shockingly, he backed up a bit. I think I surprised him. I had never talked back to him. Never. Not once. I was always afraid of what he would do to me. However, if I would have just let him hit me just once, maybe he would have been taken off to juvie or something. Everyone would have known the kind of guy he was. I never told anyone this was happening fearing that the problem would only get bigger and bigger. What kind of asshole picks on a little girl half his weight and size anyway? He stood there with his jaw open.

The guy I was with started cracking up at Tim's dumbfounded look. I had totally caught him off guard. I'm pretty sure he was expecting me to say nothing. In fact, he had a lot of nerve coming over to me and saying things to me while I was sitting there with another guy. I think he would have probably handled the situation had I not handled it myself.

"She got you!" he said while trying to contain his laughter.

Tim looked at us both for a moment, not really sure what to do and walked away. That was that. I never had to deal with him again.

Later into my adult years I discovered that his home life was a mess. His father verbally abused him and his mom. His mom was also physically abused. I'll be honest, I didn't feel bad for him. His mother, maybe, but not him. If he saw his dad say and do awful things to his mom, why did he have to do this to me? Had I known Tim was abused at home and understood all of that at the age of six, I could have told him that I felt sorry for him. It must suck to have awful parents and you had to take your frustrations out on me. If it makes you feel better to torment me then go ahead, carry on. I'll be that person for you. If only I had a ton of confidence. I allowed him to make me feel ugly. It's too bad that gaining confidence is something that takes time to attain. Thankfully, somehow years and years later I started to feel good about myself. If anyone were to say something derogatory to me today, I would have plenty to say.

Chapter 15: Let the Good Times Roll

*"If the illusion is real, let them give you a ride.
If they got thunder appeal, let them be on your side…"*

Charlene and I loved our cute little townhouse in Amherst, not too far from my parents' house. We had an understanding. Since she knew how to cook, she made all our meals and I cleaned since I loved to clean. We had it all worked out. This was a great time in our lives. We had no boyfriends, had decent paying jobs and very few bills to pay. For fun, we'd either have people over or go out to the local bars after work. Life was easy.

Charlene never went to college, but instead discovered that she had some sort of psychic ability. She would pick up office jobs, bartending and waitressing jobs from time to time, but this odd new ability started to come to the surface. It started off small. She would predict if one of her friends was pregnant, but that wasn't too hard to pull off. Then she was able to predict the sex of the baby. She actually did this a few times. She would put her hands on the mother's belly and close her eyes. She'd get real quiet and then say, "It's a girl! It's definitely a girl. I can feel it." She was never wrong.

She could also predict due dates to the hour and minute. It was crazy! She started off by predicting the sexes of the babies and due dates of just a few close friends. Then those friends started telling their friends and so on. Charlene was able to charge $100 and people would pay it just to learn the sex of their baby and their exact due date. Char's predictions were more precise than even the doctor, back in those days. Ultrasounds for every mother was not a routine procedure yet. Charlene was able to make some serious cash once word got out about her little super power.

But then her new psychic ability started to go off in a different direction. A 10 year old girl was abducted from a nearby town. Charlene loved watching murder shows, and when this little girl, Andrea Michaels made the local news, Char started paying attention. We were both parked in front of the TV every evening at 6pm just so we could hear the updates.

It started off with these strange recurring dreams. She would tell me every morning over coffee. The sun would stream through our front window. We had a cozy little table just big enough for the two of us. It was right by the window in our kitchen which was also the front of the house. There wasn't much of a view, mostly the trash cans and fields across the street, but we would meet there every morning before work for coffee. She would kick back with her long dark wavy hair up in a messy bun and smoke her cigarette. She would inhale hard and long, and then let it all out while I coughed and hacked and tried to wave the smoke away. I wasn't much of a smoker. I never got used to living with one either.

Normally we would talk about not much of anything. Sometimes we'd be so exhausted from the night before that we would just stare ahead and watch the neighbor's hummingbird feeder, depending on the season. Sometimes we'd talk about work, but our morning conversations were anything but insightful. Then the dreams started.

I don't know how long Char was having dreams about little Andrea Michaels until she finally let me in on it. In her first dream that she actually told me about, she said she kept seeing the girl with her blonde, low pigtails. She said she would see her outside on a nice, sunny day. She didn't recognize the location, not at first. She said Andrea kept running around in a circle like little kids do in a playful way. That was it, at first. Charlene had that very same dream night after night for about a week. Then really strange things started happening. In her dream, the girl started eating an ice cream cone.

"It was pink," she said.

The story was big time local news. Each morning I started writing down Charlene's dreams as she told them to me.

"Anything new today?" I'd ask?

"Not really. I keep seeing her though. Pretty clearly. She's still eating an ice cream cone. Every night. That's what she's doing. It's all over her face. It's pink," she'd tell me through exhaling out the cigarette smoke. I'd rapidly scratch down everything she said, like a reporter. I decided to try a little experiment.

"Okay, let's see if she will "tell" you something. And I don't want anything to taint your thoughts, so quit watching the news. I'll watch it and then you tell me what you dream about."

"Okay," she agreed as she tapped the ash off of her cigarette into an empty Pepsi can.

This was going to be fun, I thought, but it started to get a little scary. I watched the local news that evening. They think Andrea was taken from a shopping plaza in the next town. The reporter was talking in front of a Baskin Robbins! Holy shit!

"Char! You're not going to believe this, but they think Andrea was taken from that little shopping plaza in Westlake. We've been there. There's a Baskin Robbins there. Remember?"

"Oh shit," she said through her swigs.

"Ask her tonight if she is alive and where she is. Can you do that?" I asked, fascinated.

"I don't know. She never talks to me. I just see her getting ice cream all over her face."

"Well, try!" I demanded. Char just rolled her eyes. She was way more calm about this than I was.

The next day, she told me her dream. I pulled out my journal and started writing.

"I don't see much. She didn't tell me anything last night, but I have a feeling she is not alive. I just have this God awful feeling."

"But what did you see?" I asked, anxiously.

"She's still eating the pink ice cream, but she's in a field. There's a man in the picture, but I can't totally make it out. He looks like your dad."

What? That's so weird. My dad? What does he have to do with this?

"My dad? Hmmm. And she's still not talking to you, huh?"

"Nope," she said calmly as if her job was done.

I was absolutely baffled. Char was never around my dad, so I couldn't imagine why he was coming up in her dreams. I get why she was dreaming about Andrea Michaels. I continued to watch the news every evening to see if there were any updates. There was truly no logical explanation as to why my dad was showing up in her dreams.

I kept watching the news, and Char kept her promise. She stayed away from the TV and told everyone at work not to talk to her about the case. She never told anyone else but me about her dreams. She told her friends at work who were also obsessed with the case to leave her out of it. She told them it made her feel uncomfortable. On the news, there was nothing about a field or ice cream for days. I couldn't put it together. The dream was the same once again: the girl in a field with pink ice cream and my dad.

A few nights went by. I kept asking her during our morning coffee routine. She'd just tell me there was nothing new and to not even bother to write it down anymore. There was nothing new on the TV either.

Months went by. Eventually I stopped asking Charlene altogether. Then, in the middle of the night, Charlene woke me up and crawled into bed with me.

"I'm scared, Cyndi. Something is very wrong and it is tied to your dad. I didn't want to scare you."

I was sitting up completely awake now.

"Like you think my dad did it?" I asked. There was no way. My father would have no reason to do such a thing.

"I don't know. I see her, in a field, with your dad. She's not eating ice cream any more," she said.

"Well, what are they doing?" I asked, getting concerned.

"She looks like she's distressed. She's frightened, and I keep thinking she wants to tell me something but she never does. Your dad is just in the background, and I see a single tree. I see him walking around in the field. I can barely see him. It's a blur, but I am most certain it is him. I think we need to do something."

"Like what?" I asked.

"Well, let's go over and talk to your dad after work," she said.

"Uhm.okay."

We went back to sleep and went our separate ways in the morning. All day I couldn't help thinking about what my dad would have to do with this. We met up after work and went to my parents' house. I didn't call them ahead of time, simply because I wasn't sure what to tell them the reason for why we were coming over.

"Hey, Mom." I said when I walked in the door. She was in the kitchen cleaning up dinner. "Where's dad?"

"He's not here. He's at the farm. Why?"

My dad grew up on a farm. When I was little, and my mom worked nights, my dad would take my brother and me to my grandparent's farm where he grew up. He and my grandfather would work on the farm until late at night. My grandma would feed my brother and me and bathe us and keep us entertained. I clearly remember looking outside in the pitch black, seeing the lights of the combine, wondering when my dad was going to come in and take us home. Growing up on a farm allowed my brother and I to expand our creativity. There was an old shed that we used to play in. It was long and not very wide. The faded white paint was peeling off of it. My brother and I pretended to be pioneers and go on all sorts of adventures. They also had a gas tank to fill the tractors. It was a cylinder shape and my brother and I would ride it like it was a horse. We would spend hours using our imaginations.

"Oh, I don't know. I was just curious."

Then it dawned on me. I think it dawned on the two of us at the same time. The farm. The field. The girl. We looked at each other, dumbfounded. Leaving no explanation to my mother, we raced out the door and into the car.

"Take me there," Char demanded, pulling out a cigarette and lighting it.

"Do you have to do that in my car?" I asked, annoyed.

"Uh, yeah", she said sarcastically. "It helps me think. You want me to think or not?"

We drove in silence. I wanted nothing to disrupt her thought process. We seriously thought we were some kind of reporters or detectives or something. It was all weird and creepy, but we had nothing else to do. It was kind of fun, actually.

By the time we reached my grandmother's farm, my dad's truck was gone. I was glad for this because I wasn't sure how I would explain to him why we were there. Neither one of us had ever told anyone about our crazy little adventure. We put the car in park and the sun was just starting to go down. Char immediately got out of the car with her fingers pressed to her temples like she was trying to see something in her head. She started wandering.

"Char, look. The tree," I pointed. There was a single weeping willow tree just beyond the pond. It had been there all my life. My grandmother, brother and I would sit under that tree and feed the geese. Char started walking towards it but was shaking her head.

"This isn't it," she said, completely sure of herself. "The tree that I see is all by itself like this one, but it's in the middle of the field. This tree is just before it. The tree in my dream also isn't a weeping willow either."

"Are you sure?" I asked.

We were under the tree. It was a huge beautiful tree. I had so many good memories there. There was a soft breeze blowing the long vine like limbs causing them to calmly dance in the wind. I started walking around it while running my fingers against the bark. I was inspecting the trunk as if expecting to find a clue. There was nothing.

"Yeah, I'm sure," she said, cupping her hands around her lighter so she could light her cigarette.

Well that stinks. We got right back to the car and went home.

Once we were inside our townhouse I said, "Go to bed. Make her tell you something."

"It doesn't work that way," she said.

"Well, have you tried asking her anything in your dream?"

"Yes, but I never get anything back. Not words anyway. Just visions and feelings," she explained.

"Well, go to bed and figure it out," I commanded as I proceeded to get myself ready for bed. We were both a little frustrated that we couldn't put the clues together.

The next morning, she had a breakthrough.

"She's signing something to me," she said. "She's spelling letters with her fingers, but I don't know sign language."

Crap. Neither did I.

Since the internet wasn't a thing, we couldn't just google American Sign Language. We immediately drove off to the local library. Thankfully, it was a Saturday and we had plenty of time to sort this out. The librarian led us to a book with the signing symbols of the alphabet.

"It's too hard," Char said. "Her fingers are just making these signs, but it happens so fast. I can't make it out."

We were both disappointed. Nothing in the book was jogging her memory. All we could hope for was that she would have the dream again and that somehow she could make out the letters in her sleep. It was all getting crazy, but we both felt like we were close to getting an answer. We checked out the book and took it home.

The next morning, both of us were up early, coffee in hand, cigarette in hers.

"There's an "O" for sure," she said, making an "O" shape with her hand. "There are only 4 letters. One is an "O" and another letter is a "V". Let me see that book. I might be able to figure out another letter." I handed it to her and scooted my chair right next to hers.

"There it is. An "N". So "O", "V", and "N." That's all I got. I can't make out the last letter."

"Ovn? Von? Nov? What?"

"I don't know, but my head is hurting. I think there might be some letters missing or something. She's definitely signing 4 letters, and it's the same ones each time."

"Oven? Novice? The abbreviation for November maybe?" I said, playing around with the letters. "Maybe the letters are initials?"

"I don't know," she said. "I gotta go to work." Char was not as fascinated by her powers like I was.

Again, Charlene had the same dream over and over again for weeks. Neither one of us could figure out what the letters meant, but we both thought they had to mean something.

"Do you still see my dad in your dreams?" I asked Charlene one morning.

"Yeah, but he's just there in the background. I can see him walking back and forth or working in the field, but nothing more than that," she explained.

It's interesting how things fall into place sometimes when you least expect it. Often I would go to my parents house to print things since I didn't have my own printer. One day, I went into my dad's man cave to use his printer. My dad turned our basement into his office, but it was more like a man cave. He had a desk, a mini fridge, TV and pool table. There were photos on the wall of my brother and me. He still had the shelf my brother made in shop class back when he was in high school. I sat at his computer to bring up the document that I needed to print when something caught my eye. He had a desk calendar. I could see his schedule: Dr. appt 2pm, work at farm, pay electric bill. There it was in all caps: NOVA. It practically jumped off the page at me.

NOVA? I thought. What *is* that? I moved my papers out of the way in order to get a better look at the desk calendar. NOVA was written on his calendar once a week. I called Char.

"Could the last letter that Andrea is signing to you in your dream be an "A"?" I asked anxiously.

"I don't know," Char said. I could hear her inhale and exhale her cigarette through the phone. "Why are you asking?"

"Well, it's written all over my dad's calendar."

"Why don't you ask him what it means?" she said.

"I guess I could. But why should I tell him I'm asking? He'd think we were crazy if I told him we were trying to solve Andrea Michael's disappearance through your dreams."

"Just tell him you're curious. I mean do you have to give him an explanation?"

"I guess not. Okay, I'll go ask. See you when I get home."

My dad's evening routine was to lay on his left side on the living room floor, newspaper fanned out in front of him, with the 6 o'clock news on the TV. He did this everyday of my childhood life. I sat down on the ottoman and just blurted it out.

"Dad? What does NOVA stand for? I saw it on your calendar when I was using the printer."

"NOVA? Oh, that's where the other farm is."

Oh yeah! The other farm!

"Okay, thanks," I said and I got up quickly and left before he could ask me for an explanation. Lucky for me, my dad was never much of a conversationalist.

I drove back to our town house, probably too quickly, but I wanted to tell Charlene what I found out to her face and right away. I ran up the stairs and burst through her bedroom door.

"The word she is spelling to you is NOVA," I said, out of breath.

"NOVA? What the f--- is that?" Char asked.

"It's my dad's other farm. My dad owns a 2nd farm. I forgot. Growing up we always called it "the other farm." NOVA is where it is located. Do you think that has anything to do with Andrea Michaels?"

"No idea."

"I mean, maybe we should call the tip line. Don't you think?"

"They would never believe me. I have no idea how that could be tied to her," she said.

"Well, get in bed and dream. Maybe she will tell you more."

"I don't know Cyn. This could all just be coincidental."

Char went to bed that night. We woke up the next morning like clock work. She had my coffee waiting and was already smoking away.

"I think I will call the police tip line," she said calmly. "I mean, what do I have to lose?"

"Well, now I don't know. What if they think you did it? I mean, how would you explain how you know?"

"I could tell the truth, you know."

"True." I said. "Why the change of mind?"

"Because she's there," she said, very seriously.

"How do you know? What did you see?"

Charlene nor myself had never been to the other farm in our lives.

"In my dream there is a tree. She's sitting against it," she started, as I pulled out my journal and a pen.

"She's curled up in a ball. In a fetal position," she said, closing her eyes. She continually dragged on her cigarette. "There's mud on her face and she's crying," she paused. "The tears are blood. But there is blood all around her. She's lying in it. I'm scared. But I have a really sick feeling. I know she's there. I know it."

"Should we go there?" I asked nervously. I knew I would need to tell my dad though because I would need to ask him how to get there.

"No. We should call the tip line."

"Okay, I said, as I turned on the TV.

We sat in our living room and waited to see if there were any new updates in the case. Normally they would put the tip line on the screen for viewers to call if they had any leads. The case was kind of dying down. It had been months and there hadn't been any new leads. There wasn't much to report. Today was no different. There was nothing on the news about Andrea Michaels. I turned off the TV, disappointed.

"What should we do?" I said. "Should I just ask my dad to take us there?"

"No. You don't want to see what is there. I'm just going to call the police. I know if I don't, I'm going to have this dream either for the rest of my life or until she is found.

I don't want to keep seeing this and maybe coming forward will help it go away."

Char picked up the phone as if it was her civic duty to do so. I heard her explain the absolute truth: she was a psychic and she had recurring dreams. She told them about the log I had been keeping. I heard her give her our phone number. Then she hung up.

"Well??? What did they say?"

"They said they had no other leads, so they are going now to take a look."

"You've got to be kidding me."

"Nope. They told me to stay by the phone in case they need more information."

We went about our day. She went to work, and I went to school for my part time job as a tutor. My classroom phone rang. It was the secretary.

"You have a call from a Charlene. You want me to put her through?" Char never calls me at work. Something's wrong, I thought.

"Yes, yes please put her through. I'll take the call." I shushed my students.

"The cops are coming to pick me up. Couldn't find anything from what I told them. They want me to go there with them."

"You're kidding me. Should I meet you out there?"

"No. You don't want to see what I can see. IF I lead them there, and IF they find something, you don't want to be there for it. Trust me."

"Okay," I said. I was unable to concentrate for the rest of the day.

I went home to our empty townhouse and warmed up some food Char left for me in the fridge. I turned on the TV.

"Up next...Police follow a tip on the disappearance of Andrea Michaels," the reporter on the TV said. Then it went to a commercial.

Holy crap.

After the commercial, there was a policeman doing a miniature press conference. He was on a podium with about 4 or 5 reporters surrounding him, all holding their microphones near his face. I could see a field in the background.

"We have found a body. We think it might be Andrea Michaels, but that remains to be confirmed."

The crowd of reporters all started speaking at once. One reporter's voice rose above all the others.

"Who gave you the tip?" she asked.

"We aren't going to say at this time," he said.

Reporters started swarming him and were talking all at once. He walked off the podium. About an hour later, Char walked through the door and collapsed on the couch.

"Hand me my lighter," she said, before I could even get a word in. "Thank God you didn't go. I know you want me to tell you, but it's pretty bad."

"Uh yeah. Just tell me. I'll be fine."

"You probably won't be fine. I definitely am not, but I will tell you because I know you aren't going to let it go.

She was right.

"The police were not looking in the right place. They kept searching the forest around the field. I told them I saw a single tree. We went from field to field. It was never the right spot. Then they drove me around in the back of the cop car. A sick feeling came over my entire body. I told them we were close. I cannot believe that they listened to what I was saying, but I guess when you have nothing, an amature psychic will do."

I chuckled, sitting on the edge of my seat, hanging on her every word.

"We found one more field. It was the one owned by your dad. If only I had known the exact location in the first place, I could have led them there faster. In hindsight, we should have told your dad. There were two trees all by themselves in the field. They were yards apart. Of course we went to the wrong tree first. There was nothing. So I hiked my ass all the way over to the other tree and you'll never believe what we saw."

"WHAT?" I said. She wasn't getting the words out fast enough.

"In the distance I saw something like a tarp or a blanket or something. I could see it blowing in the wind. It didn't look like much until we got closer. It was a towel that was tucked underneath the body. I watched the police slowly reveal what was underneath."

"What was it?"

"I only caught a glimpse. It was definitely a human body. It was partially decomposed" she said, wincing. "Once I saw it was a body, I couldn't look. The glimpse that I saw was enough for me. I don't know how they do what they do. I can't say much more. Just know it was a child's body. Okay? I don't want to say anything else out loud. I sat in the car while they removed it. It took forever."

A few days went by and it was confirmed. The body Char helped the police find was indeed Andrea's body.

The next few days and weeks were a whirlwind for Charlene. Once word got out that she was able to find the body of a missing child, the media went crazy. They were calling her and me. Reporters were showing up at the house. Neither one of us had expected any of this. Charlene did not like all of the attention. We even had Nate stay with us until things calmed down. He was happy to go out the front door and tell the reporters to leave. People were willing to pay big bucks for her to tell parents where their missing children were. Charlene didn't take a dime. In fact, she turned every single person away, except for Oprah, which is the vessel she was able to use to get people off of her back.

Oprah Winfrey had a special episode which included several psychics including the world famous psychic Sylvia Brown. I was shocked that Charlene was invited to be on this show.

Charlene walked Oprah and the audience through the recurring dreams she had about Andrea Michaels. She also told them about how I would write everything down and she would not watch the news at all. I only got to sit in the audience, but I have to admit, it was pretty cool, even though I never actually got to meet Oprah if you were wondering. Charlene perfectly articulated her reasons for never taking a dime and that her days as a psychic were over.

"Why is it, Charlene, that you don't want to continue. You could help dozens of families across the world," Oprah asked her.

"Because I can't. I don't have any more dreams. And I don't want to have them. It is scary. This started off as two friends kind of playing around, but then things got real. I never asked for this. I was only able to predict the sexes of my friends' babies and when they were going to be born. That's it. I have grown up watching murder mysteries most of my life. It's just the kind of TV I enjoy watching. I don't know why Andrea decided to speak to me, but I never want to do this again," she explained.

She needed a cigarette. I could tell.

"I mean, I could have been wrong," she continued. "What if someone asks me if their child is alive or dead? The truth is, I don't know. If I was wrong, I couldn't live with myself. I only went to the police because there were no other leads. I really don't think I can do this again."

And that was it. She never had any dreams about missing kids. She never had any feelings about missing kids. It was over. No one even bothered her anymore. She did what she was supposed to do. She was brave and a hero in my eyes. Sometimes, you just have to speak up, no matter how crazy it may sound.

Chapter 16: You Might Think

"But somewhere sometimes, when you're curious, I'll be back around..."

To recap, Amy took off to California. We would write letters back and forth to each other, but eventually, things started settling down for her. She found an office job and a really great guy.

Char later moved in with a guy she met at the bar. We actually still lived in the same town and would get together for lunch from time to time, but you know how it goes. We grow up, we move out and start branching off onto our own paths.

Viv was still living in Arizona when we got the news about Samson. The summer that Samson stole that case of pop would be the last time I would see him. That was the same summer that Viv spent without Terrence. It was the first summer we actually had together with no boyfriends. Viv and I, and often Char and Amy would spend time with Samson and his friend Rex. Like I said, there was never much to do, so most of our days were spent driving around, getting fast food or hanging out at my parent's pool.

One day at the end of that summer while we were hanging out at my parents' pool, out of nowhere, Samson told us he was leaving for the army in 2 days. I knew he was going to go into the army, but I never knew when he was actually leaving. He just kind of sprung the news upon all of us.

"No you're not," I said, jokingly, sipping my Mcdonald's Pepsi from earlier that day.

"Yeah, I am," he insisted. I just didn't really believe him. He joked around a lot.

"Okay, so where will you be stationed?" I asked, assuming he'd make something up.

"Saudi," he said, getting kind of serious.

"As in Arabia?" Char asked.

"Yeah," he said, looking down. "As in Saudi Arabia. I'll be fighting in Desert Storm." We all looked at Rex to confirm. He sat there, looking very serious and shrugged his shoulders.

"I still don't believe you," I said.

"Okay. That's cool," Samson said, lighting a cigarette.

"Okay, well, if you are really leaving, then I'm going to ask my mom to make you a going away dinner then," I said, jokingly, but testing him as well. I knew he would not want my mother to go through all that trouble if he wasn't really leaving.

"Go ahead. I'd love that," he said, cigarette dangling from his lips.

"Okay, I will." I started getting up slowly, giving him more than enough time to stop me.

"I'm walking away now, Samson. I'm getting closer to the door," I said, in a sing songy tone.

He just nodded his head as the rest of them watched.

"I've got my hand on the door, Samson. You can stop me any time," I taunted.

"Oh my gosh. You're serious," I stopped.

The next day, my mom made him a delicious steak and baked potato dinner. We were all there: my parents and my brother, Amy, Viv, Charlene, Rex and me. Samson was being his normal self, cracking jokes here and there. It was like he wasn't really leaving, and I didn't totally believe him anyway. I had never met Samson's parents, and then it dawned on me. Why wasn't his mom doing this for him? My mom pulled out a cake and some small plates. The cake said, "Best of Luck Samson" and it had the American flag on the cake. Samson teared up and thanked everyone.

It was really a nice little party. I don't think any of us truly understood where Samson was headed, except for maybe my dad, who was also in the army before I was born. But as usual, my dad didn't say much of anything. We each wrote down our addresses so Samson could write to us all and let us know he got there okay. We gave him hugs and everyone went home. It was more like a small birthday party if anything.

The next morning was a Saturday. I looked at the clock. It was 10am. I knew Samson was probably on his way to the airport. His flight was to leave at noon. It was a pretty normal Saturday. I had my Kellogg's Frosted Mini Wheats and ice water. I turned on the TV to watch Pee Wee's playhouse, and yes, although I was going to be a senior in high school, I truly did get a kick out of this show. Later in the day, Viv walked over and we sat in my room and painted our nails.

"I wonder where Samson is right now," Viv said.

"I think he said he was flying into the Newark Airport and then off to Saudi," I said.

Neither of us knew much about Desert Storm. Samson didn't tell us what he would be doing there either. I don't think he knew. Viv and I never watched the news. Samson leaving was just all so sudden. We heard the doorbell ring, but our nails were wet, so neither one of us got up. I heard my brother let whoever it was into the house. A few seconds later, my bedroom door opened. It was Rex, followed by Samson's sister Kristen and then, there was Samson.

"What the???" I said, super confused. "I thought you left?"

"Well, I was supposed to, but I don't want to go," Samson said, oddly surprisingly calmly.

"Don't you have to?" Viv asked.

"I do," he said.

"Well, why are you here then?" I asked, curiously.

"He wouldn't let me drive him to the airport," Rex said.

"What do you mean he wouldn't let you? Samson, aren't you going to get in trouble?" Viv asked.

"I don't know. Maybe. I was thinking I could just hang out here for a little while."

"Samson? Are you crazy? I'm pretty sure if you signed up for this, you're going to have to go."

"Well, I changed my mind. I don't want to go."

"Did you talk to anyone about this? Don't you have a recruiting officer that you have to talk to?" I asked.

"Yeah, but I don't want to talk to him."

Oh my gosh! What was going on here? I felt like we were going to get into some kind of trouble, like bad trouble with the United States Army for hiding a fugitive. I wasn't sure what to do. We were all just kids. What did we know? Samson literally had no plan of action. He just simply didn't show up for the flight. You would think someone would be looking for him by now. It was way past his flight departure.

We didn't know what else to do so we did what any other group of teenagers would do who was hiding a friend from going to Saudi Arabia: we went into the basement and played pool. Eventually, things were kind of normal and none of us talked about Samson leaving for the army. My parents liked for everyone to leave at midnight, so they did. Viv went home and I went to bed.

Sunday evening rolled around and I saw headlights in my driveway. I pulled the curtain over to the side so I could see out the window. It was Rex. It was dark and rainy and I saw Rex get out of the car holding a shopping bag over his head to keep himself from getting wet.

"We have to go to the airport. The recruiter got a hold of Samson. If he doesn't go, he's going to have to pay a hefty fine. You wanna come with us?"

"Yeah, I suppose. Let me tell my parents and get my shoes on." I hopped in the back with Samson's sister, Kristen. She had been crying, I could tell.

No one spoke for the entire ride. It was raining and dark, and this time, the weather seemed to match the mood. I can't imagine what Samson must have been thinking. No one knew how to break the silence, so no one did. All I could do was watch the rain drops drip down the window.

When we got to the passenger drop off gate, we all got out. Samson had just a small bag. He grabbed his sister and I and gave us a long, tight hug. His sister was sobbing uncontrollably. She grabbed his face and said, "Just come home."

It was agonizing. I knew he needed to go. I took Kristen's hand in mine and led her back inside the car so we wouldn't get too wet. I saw Samson shake Rex's hand and then pull him in for a hug too. As Rex walked back into the car, I saw him wipe away a tear from his eyes. We all sat in the car while the automatic doors to the airport opened up and swallowed Samson into the abyss called the real world. I sat right next to Kristen. She put her head on my shoulder and the two of us cried all the way back to Amherst.

Chapter 17: Since I Held You

"I won't forget the way you said it doesn't bother you much..."

Since Samson was now in Saudi, I started paying attention to the news. My dad watched it religiously at 6pm while laying on his side in the middle of the living room. We were never allowed to watch anything else at 6pm. This was my dad's time. I never watched the news, which was probably why it was so shocking to us that there was even a war brewing over in the Middle East.

It was now January, 1991. Samson had been gone since the end of August. We received a few letters from him. We'd send him photos of us. He seemed to be okay. He missed us all, of course, but otherwise, he seemed to be doing fine. However, the evening news would prove otherwise. Iraq had sent missiles into Saudi Arabia. There were explosions all over the TV. I gasped.

"Dad, is that where Samson is?" I couldn't believe what I was seeing.

"Yes. He's over there somewhere, but that doesn't mean he's in the middle of all of that," he explained, pointing at the TV. I have never seen much emotion from my dad. I wasn't sure how he was sitting there unmoved by what we were watching.

"Dad? Is Samson going to come home?" I asked, concerned.

"Well, so far, there are no US casualties, so that's good. He's probably not going to come home anytime soon though," he said, trying to be positive.

I sat there for the rest of the evening and watched it all unfold. No wonder Samson didn't want to go. All he knew was small town life. I don't think Samson ever left Ohio even. How in the world was he going to live through this? If I was rattled by watching it on TV, I can only imagine his mental state being in that mess.

I kept writing and writing Samson. I wrote a letter a day, begging him to write us back and just let us know that he was fine. Days and weeks went by and we heard nothing.

We finally heard back from him in June. He was home, but "home" was not Amherst, Ohio. He was stationed in North Carolina. He spent his time in Saudi as an IED which stands for Improvised Explosive Device Specialist, which meant he had to look for bombs and get rid of them. Holy Hell. I knew Samson, and those months in Saudi had to have messed with his head.

Viv and I graduated in 1992. Char graduated in 1993. Amy and I went off to college. Viv was off in Arizona. Charlene and I lived together for about a year during our "detective years". After that, we all kind of lost touch. I moved back home with my parents. One day when I got home from work, my mom said that I had a message from Kristen.

"Kristen? Kristen who?" It had been years.

"I think it's Samson's sister Kristen."

That's odd. Kristen and I were never friends. It's not that we were enemies or anything. She was just Samson's sister. She never hung out with us. The most time I had ever spent with her was way back in the 90's when we were in the back of Rex's car, dropping Samson off at the airport.

"Here's her number," my mom said, handing me a small piece of paper.

I took it from her hand, feeling very concerned. I was surprised that Kristen even knew where to get a hold of me. I dialed the number on the paper.

"Kristen? It's Cyndi. Is everything okay? My mom said you called."

"I have some unfortunate news," she said, her voice shaky. "Samson committed suicide."

I had to sit down. I couldn't believe what I was hearing.

"When did this happen?" I asked, still in complete shock.

"About 2 weeks ago. We are going to receive his body by the end of the week. We will be having calling hours this Saturday," she said.

The last time I heard the word "body" in reference to a dead body was when Michaela passed away. Hearing your friend is now just "a body" is a hard pill to swallow.

"Can you get a hold of everyone? I have no idea where all of his friends are. I figured your parents lived in the same house, so I found their number in the phonebook, but I don't know how to reach the rest of his friends. I found Rex and told him, and now you."

"Uhm, yes, of course. I can do that," I said, still in shock.

"Okay, thanks. I will call you when I know more," she said.

"Wait. Do you know why? Did he leave a letter or anything?" I asked.

"They didn't tell me anything. I just know that his body will be here either Thursday or Friday."

I sat at the kitchen table. I was sitting next to the very spot where Samson sat when we gave him his last home cooked meal. I still have that photo of him.

I called Viv, Charlene and Amy. Viv flew in from Arizona and Amy came in from California. Charlene and I saw each other from time to time, but neither one of us had seen Viv or Amy in about 2 or 3 years. It's too bad that it took the death of someone we loved for us to get together again, but I guess that's just how life goes.

The four of us met at the funeral home for Samson's closed casket calling hours. Just like Michaela's calling hours, there were poster boards of photos and then up near the casket was a picture of Samson in his Class A uniform. I had never seen this photo before.

He was an 18 year old boy when we dropped him off at the airport. In this photo, he looked like he was in his mid 30's. I searched his eyes for that small town boy that we knew and loved. Where was the kid that stole the case of pop way back when? What did Desert Storm do to him?

The four of us edged our way to the front. None of us had much to say other than we were shocked at the news. Samson didn't write to any of us any more and we just simply lost touch. Never in our lives did we think the Samson would do something like this. He was happy and goofy and his goal all the time was to make us laugh.

There were people standing at the front near his casket . The American flag was draped over top. When I got to the front, I realized how little I knew about Samson.

I assumed it was his family that was standing there, only because I saw Kristen, but I didn't recognize anyone else. All the time that Samson and I were friends, I had never been to his house. He was always at mine. I assumed that the older lady standing next to Kristen was their mom, but it was kind of hard to tell. You would think the mother of the deceased would be obvious, but not this time.

When I got to Kristen, I gave her a big hug and she started shaking with tears. I barely knew her. My only memory of her was when we dropped him off to the airport when he was deployed. Somewhere along that thirty minute drive, we bonded in the silence.

I didn't know what to say other than, "I'm so sorry." I had a million questions, but I could tell that this was not the time to ask. I wanted to know why he would do something like this. Was it all just too much? I couldn't imagine the things he saw or had to do when he was overseas. Samson was like me. Living in a small town felt safe. We were clueless about what the outside world might be like. I longed for the days when we had to find ways to keep ourselves entertained. There was one question that I asked Kristen simply because I was dying to know.

"Kristen," I whispered into her ear. "Is that lady your mom?" She nodded, but looked a little disgusted.

"What about that man over there?" I kind of nodded my head in his direction so I wouldn't be too obvious. "Is that your dad?"

She shook her head. "Cousins," she said, and looked down.

Very interesting. Samson never mentioned his mom. As far as I knew, he didn't live with her. It always seemed like him and Kristen lived on their own without parents. Looking back, I cannot believe I never asked.

Amy and Viv started talking to Kristen. I nudged Charlene in her side to get her attention. I whispered, "That's his mom."

She looked at me like she was kind of pissed off at seeing her. Did she know something that I didn't?

It was our turn to say something to his mother, but I was kind of confused. She wasn't crying like Kristen had been. She didn't even have tears in her eyes or anything. Unable to hide my confusion, I walked up to her and extended my hand. Not really knowing what to say, I introduced myself and told her I was friends with Samson in high school.

"You're Samson's mom?" I asked. She smiled and nodded. She looked at Charlene which was also a signal that I should move along. Char did not extend her hand. Instead she glared at her. She made eye contact with her as she walked by. Somehow she managed to lock eyes with his mother, not breaking her glare until she was several steps past her. It was as if Char's body language was telling her to watch her back. Strange.

When we got to the casket, I put my hand on top of the flag. All I could do was cry and shake my head in disbelief. Charlene could not keep it together. She was audibly crying, but not making a scene or anything. Amy rushed over and put her arm around her. Viv and I stepped away and let them have a moment. Charlene knew something that the rest of us didn't know. There was a crowd gathering, waiting their turn to go up to the casket. Viv and I decided to go outside and wait for Amy and Charlene.

We leaned up against Viv's rental car. "Did you see that? Did you see Char glare at his mom?" I asked her.

"I did!" she said, as shocked as I was.

"What do you think that was all about?"

"No clue," she said. "Let's ask her when she gets out here." It seemed like forever for Charlene and Amy to reach our cars.

"What the heck was that all about?" I asked Charlene.

"Samson's mom was never really a mom, you know," she explained, wiping her nose with a tissue. "You ever hear him talk about her? Or his dad?"

"No," I said, and Viv shook her head.

"You ever wonder why you and Rex and Kristen took him to the airport and not his mother?" she said, pissed.

Actually I had. I just never asked.

"She didn't give a shit about those two. How dare she show up here?" Char said, getting worked up again. "She was never there! If she was, then she was passed out or drunk. She was never a mother," she said, sniffling. "Cyn, think about it. She showed up here simply so she could get all those military benefits. She doesn't deserve any of it. All of it should go to Kristen, not her," she continued. "Honestly, I want to go in there and kick her ass."

Charlene was a fighter. She was that kind of friend that you wanted on your side. There was nothing sugar coated about Char. She would call it like she saw it everytime, and she never cared what other people thought. If you were being an ass, she would tell you. And if you wronged her family or friends, she would call you out for sure. We knew it was time to go. This was not the time or place for Charlene to call out Samson's mom. We loaded up in our cars and left.

Samson's funeral was the next day. It was a beautiful spring afternoon in May. There were no clouds in the sky and the sun felt warm, considering we hadn't had a day warm enough to be outside comfortably in a long time. When we arrived, we saw Samson's casket under the canopy with the American flag still draped over top. A small crowd of close friends and family were gathered in chairs. Because his casket was closed for the calling hours, I felt somewhat disconnected, as if none of this was really happening. After the minister read the eulogy, two military representatives folded the flag neatly in half and then into a tight triangle.

"On behalf of the President of the United States, the United States Army, and a grateful nation, please accept this flag as a symbol of our appreciation for your loved one's honorable and faithful service."

One of the representatives handed the folded flag to Samson's mother. I glanced over at Charlene and she rolled her eyes. She pulled out a cigarette and lit it. She took a long drag while tears silently flowed from her eyes.

After the service, people stood around talking. We caught up with Rex and asked him when was the last time he heard from Samson and why he would do such a thing.

"He wrote to me a few times while he was still in Saudi and then once letting me know he was stationed at Fort Bragg, North Carolina, but other than that, nothing," Rex explained.

"So you have no idea why he would do this?" Amy asked.

"No. I wish I did. I wish I could tell you more, but I really don't know."

While we were talking Kristen came over to us. She had a large, gold shipping envelope in her hands. The envelope was already torn open at the top. I recognized the handwriting right away. The envelope was from Samson.

"This came in the mail the other day," she said, handing the envelope to Viv. Viv glanced around at us, shocked and confused. "What is it?" she asked.

"Open it," Kristen said.

Viv pulled out 5 unopened, white business sized envelopes. Each one had our name on it in Samson's writing. She passed out the envelopes to each of us. We held them in our hands, stunned. Char took hers and walked away. I saw her sit on a bench a few yards away. I saw her open her letter. As she read it, she pulled out some tissues and began wiping her face.

The rest of us didn't know what to do. I wanted to open it, but I didn't want to all at once. We were all looking at Charlene's reaction to decide what to do. I decided to sit at the bench that was right where we were standing.

"How about on the count of 3, we all open our letters together?" Rex suggested. We all nodded.

"1.2.3..." he said.

Chapter 18: Everything You Say

*"But then you tell me that you can't go on
And you think you're losing sight..."*

Cyn,

It's been a long time, hasn't it? I am writing to you because you were such a significant person in my life and I know I owe you an explanation. When I wrote to you so long ago, I was not okay. I just knew you would worry if I told you otherwise. You didn't need to know about the things that were happening over there and all the awful things I saw. You were just a kid and so was I. I never had the chance to thank you for all the good times. Hanging out with you, Viv, Amy and Char that summer was the best summer of my life. The meal your mom prepared for me before I left meant a ton to me. You are lucky to have parents like yours. I'm just in a real dark place right now. I hope you'll be able to understand. I just can't explain it. I know you're probably pissed at me, so to make you laugh, here is a copy of my best poem, your favorite, The Virgin Stripper. See if you can get it published. Who knows you might make a buck or two. You know how it is, things are worth more when you're dead, ha ha. And if you ever find dimes, think of me. I left them for you. Don't hate me, Samson

The Virgin Stripper by Samson
She dazzles in the night
Blinded by the light
She's an angel during the day
Foolin' everyone at night
She's strutting on stage
In a thong that's beige
Never really feeling love
She's as precious as a dove.

Even though there were tears rolling down my face, all of our faces for that matter, I couldn't help but chuckle. Dammit, Samson, I thought to myself. I would have given anything to go back in time. I kissed my index finger and pressed it to his signature. I looked down at my feet, and to my surprise, there was a shiny dime.

The end.

Afterword

I've always wanted to write a novel. In my spare time my husband and I make up silly stories that will probably never be published. Just for fun, we came up with a story about Morty the Confused Duck, for example. Morty is confused because he lives in the state of Ohio where the weather is rather confusing. He can't figure out when the best time is to migrate his flock south. This causes all sorts of stress. His flock is losing faith in him. His wife is concerned that the guys don't invite him over for cards any more.

I've noticed that everything, for me, becomes a story. So many adventures have formed in my mind just from simply existing. Once, a student of mine was looking at his reflection in a puddle during recess. A story formed in my mind about gnomes who live in the underworld, yet control the entire world. The only way they can get ideas into the human world is through puddles. There's stress among the gnome world. They get separated from their families if they can't get us to follow through. They have meetings about when the next rain will come and how they will get our attention.

This is how my mind works. Everything, and I mean everything, can be turned into a story. I am a 5th grade Social Studies and Science teacher. Everytime I teach something, yet another story forms in my head. I have a children's story about food chains, another story about a Native American themed camp where parents can drop their children off to live like the Native Americans for the week, and another book to help people plan what to wear daily. I'll call it something like "Spirit Week for the Whole Year."

It's kind of cool to be inspired constantly, but it's also sometimes very annoying.

All of these stories are fighting each other in my mind. I am their vessel into this world. Often I feel a constant nagging in my head. "Write me!" They say. "It's my turn!" They begged me.

A friend of mine knew that I had this strange, story writing urge. She introduced me to NaNoWriMo which stands for National Novel Writing Month. This organization challenges writers of all levels to write a novel in 30 days during the month of November. I put the challenge on the back burner for years, but for whatever reason, I decided to participate in the challenge this year, 2021. I actually won it, if you can believe that, with this very story. This, my friends, is what roughly 50,000 words looks like.

I have never written a book or even a short story on a sheet of notebook paper. Thus far, all of my silly stories have lived only in my head. Initially, when I took the challenge, I had no idea what I would write about. I simply sat at my laptop on November first and I started to type. "Who's Gonna Drive You Home" was born.

I have no idea why this is the story that came out. It was never in my mind. Honestly, the gnome underworld story was the story that had been bothering my soul since last year, desperately wanting to come out. I thought for sure that's the novel that would have been born into the world through me, but that was not the case. If anything, "Who's Gonna Drive You Home" might help someone maybe? I'm not really sure. It definitely helped me to put a lot of my past into perspective. It's likely that may be the only reason it needed to be written. I might have written it for myself. But here is, in print for you to enjoy as well. I hope you did. Don't tell me if you didn't. Don't tell me how awful my punctuation is. Only tell me if you liked it. If you've never written a book before, it is absolutely terrifying to allow someone else to read it.

People say writing a novel is a lot like having a baby and it is true. Once that baby starts growing inside you, there's no turning back, especially if you have already told people about it. After the baby is inside for long enough, it wants to come out. That's what it's like to write a novel. Like having a child, there is never going to be a good time for that to happen.

Made in the USA
Middletown, DE
03 March 2023

26072132R00116